Hedge Accounting Unlocked

The Essential Guide for CFOs

KEVIN MITCHELL
FCCA, CA, AMCT, CCTA

Praise

"I'm delighted to witness the release of 'Hedge Accounting Unlocked'. As a mentor of Kevin, I've had the privilege of observing his growth and expertise in the field of hedge accounting. This book is a testament to his dedication to assisting financial leaders in navigating this complex domain. Kevin's practical insights, as demonstrated through the 'HEDGEHOG Method,' showcase his deep knowledge and ability to communicate complex concepts clearly. He has not only simplified a difficult subject in a very readable fashion but also provided valuable templates and real-world case studies, making this book a valuable resource for finance professionals in SME's. 'Hedge Accounting Unlocked' reflects Kevin's passion for empowering others in the finance world. It delivers a very high ROI to the reader, and I believe it could significantly help smaller companies manage, and especially account, for their financial risk. I'm pleased to have played a small part in Kevin's journey."

- Paul Nailand, Co-Founder, Visual Risk

"Having worked closely with Kevin over many years, I have seen his appreciation of the technical and practical problems faced by accounting professionals on treasury issues develop to a very high level. Hedge Accounting Unlocked is the culmination of these years of advising corporate clients on hedge accounting standards, with a strong understanding of the real day-to-day difficulties and highly relevant, practical solutions that are required. The case studies and templates will be an enormous benefit to all accounting professionals and go a long way to simplifying the complex world of treasury accounting".

- Derek Mumford, Consultant, Rochford Capital

"I have been in Treasury Quantitative Risk Compliance and Governance for over 30 years, and I highly recommend "Hedge Accounting Unlocked" as an essential addition to any Treasury Executives toolkit or Accountant's bookshelf. Kevin is a Hedge Accounting domain expert, and via his step-by-step HEDGEHOG methodology, he has managed to convey complex statutory obligations in a relatively straightforward manner. I love the war stories, as non-compliance often has unforeseen far-reaching consequences. His book also includes very helpful templates to assist you in meeting minimum obligations with traceability and auditability. A Warning - if you follow Kevin's HEDGEHOG methodology, a Zen-like confidence in your Hedge Accounting practices and compliance may result!"

- John Miller, Director, bbAppLabs Pty Ltd

"Well, well, look who's gone and written a book! As Kevin's friend and fellow accountant, I'm thrilled to endorse his latest work, 'Hedge Accounting Unlocked.' Kevin's practical insights are a testament to his deep understanding of the intricate world of hedge accounting - a tricky and complex topic for us CFOs!"

- Mark Kinchin, CFO, Safewill

Contents

Dedication

I want to express my appreciation to those who have played a significant role in my journey in finance. Your support and influence on my career have been invaluable.

To my valued clients, your trust and continued partnership have fuelled my passion for hedge accounting. Working with each of you has been a pleasure, and I am deeply grateful for the opportunities provided to me. To my colleagues, thank you for your camaraderie, memorable moments, and dedication.

To my mentors and managers, your guidance and willingness to share your wisdom and time have been instrumental in my professional development. Your support during my early days as an accountant laid the foundation for my journey.

Lastly, but most importantly, I want to express my profound gratitude to my family. My parents, in-laws, and wife have been my unwavering support system. Your belief in me and your understanding has made all the difference. To my beautiful wife, thank you for being my rock, my voice of reason, and putting up with my endless discussions about hedge accounting for over a decade!

This book, 'Hedge Accounting Unlocked', is dedicated to each of you as a token of my appreciation and a celebration of your impact on my journey.

Introduction

Welcome to a tailored guide written explicitly for CFOs using financial derivatives to manage market risks such as foreign exchange, interest rates, and commodity prices. I'm Kevin Mitchell, a skilled hedge accounting specialist with over ten years of experience advising CFOs of listed companies across APAC and Europe. Every month, I engage in meticulous reporting on billions in hedging activity to help ensure that my clients avoid unwarranted accounting volatility.

As a Chief Financial Officer, your role is vital in safeguarding and enhancing critical financial metrics. This book is designed to give you practical insights into running an effective hedge accounting program and includes an in-depth exploration of the HEDGEHOG Method. This comprehensive methodology offers guidance on optimising eight hedge accounting topics, providing a tailored solution for busy, time-constrained CFOs like yourself.

This book can also help you identify potential gaps and opportunities within your business and team to streamline the accounting process for financial derivatives. With so many demanding responsibilities and accounting standards to adhere to, it's not practical to delve into the nitty-gritty of every accounting standard. I'll focus on the essential areas every CFO must know, saving you valuable time (and stress!) during month-end processes.

One of the biggest challenges for CFOs is managing budget allocation. While budget constraints require careful selection and scrutiny of available options, your ultimate goal is to ensure financial reporting accuracy and achieve a clean audit with no last-minute surprises. Therefore, selecting the best value-for-money infrastructure is essential for your company's financial health and to safeguard your personal brand. As someone who values working smarter, not harder, I'll share insights from my career to emphasise the importance of seeking assistance, leveraging automation, and implementing effective systems to streamline processes.

By immersing yourself in this book, utilising real case studies and my downloadable resources, you'll upskill your knowledge, boost confidence, and enhance your value as a crucial asset to your business.

So, let's dive in and take your hedge accounting program to the next level!

The HEDGEHOG Method

The HEDGEHOG Method addresses eight key areas to optimise hedge accounting programs and ensure compliance with accounting standards. My comprehensive methodology empowers organisations to establish effective policies, streamline processes, and optimise financial reporting. By combining this framework with my advisory experience, I have successfully tackled various business and hedge accounting challenges.

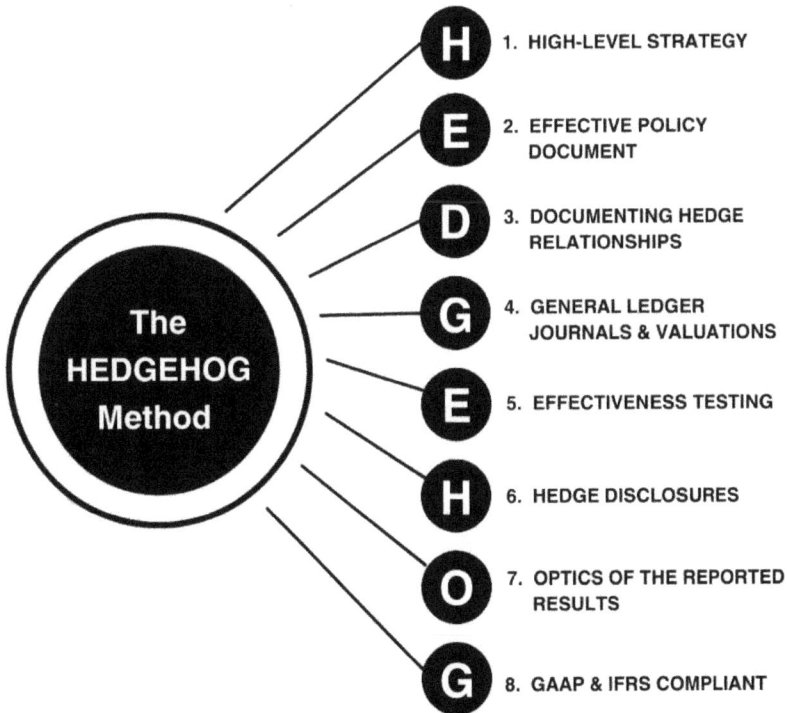

The HEDGEHOG Method

- **H** 1. HIGH-LEVEL STRATEGY
- **E** 2. EFFECTIVE POLICY DOCUMENT
- **D** 3. DOCUMENTING HEDGE RELATIONSHIPS
- **G** 4. GENERAL LEDGER JOURNALS & VALUATIONS
- **E** 5. EFFECTIVENESS TESTING
- **H** 6. HEDGE DISCLOSURES
- **O** 7. OPTICS OF THE REPORTED RESULTS
- **G** 8. GAAP & IFRS COMPLIANT

Part One

The first section of this book contains steps 1 and 2 of the HEDGEHOG Method, High-Level Strategy and the Effective Policy Document.

Refraining from establishing a clear risk management strategy that runs in parallel with the accounting treatment and overall business objectives is one you want to avoid as a CFO. It's essential for any organisation to get clear on the accounting policy and the objectives and have these documented and readily available. This section provides an excellent overview of hedge accounting, which will be helpful for readers less familiar with the types of hedge relationships that exist and will aid the understanding of the remainder of the book.

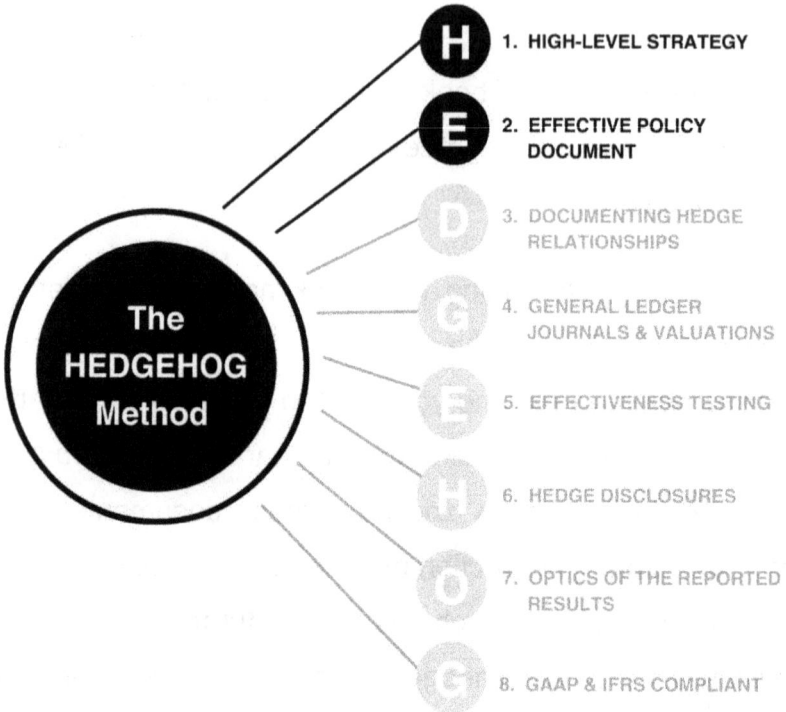

H 1. **HIGH-LEVEL STRATEGY**

E 2. **EFFECTIVE POLICY DOCUMENT**

D 3. DOCUMENTING HEDGE RELATIONSHIPS

G 4. GENERAL LEDGER JOURNALS & VALUATIONS

E 5. EFFECTIVENESS TESTING

H 6. HEDGE DISCLOSURES

O 7. OPTICS OF THE REPORTED RESULTS

G 8. GAAP & IFRS COMPLIANT

The HEDGEHOG Method

Chapter 1:
High-Level Strategy

Introduction

This chapter provides an introductory understanding of hedge accounting, its benefits, and the different types of hedge relationships. It aims to equip CFOs, particularly those new to hedge accounting, with the fundamental principles to navigate this complex financial practice. By familiarising themselves with these concepts, CFOs can enhance the accuracy of their company's financial position and performance representation.

The chapter begins by outlining the overarching principle of the International Financial Reporting Standard (IFRS) 9, which enables companies to offset gains or losses from financial instruments used to manage risks, such as foreign exchange rate fluctuations, commodity price movements, or interest rate changes. It emphasises the importance of meticulous documentation and analysis to ensure compliance with hedge accounting standards. The three main types of hedge relationships are introduced: cash flow hedge, fair value hedge, and net investment hedge. The most common type (cash flow hedge) is further discussed, illustrating how it is used to manage cash flow variability resulting from changes in the fair value of assets, liabilities, or forecasted transactions. The chapter also explains how cash flow hedges can reduce volatility in profit or loss by parking unrealised gains or losses on foreign exchange contracts into a cash flow hedge reserve.

The section titled 'Strategy and Objectives' stresses the significance of a clear and well-defined hedge accounting strategy. It advises CFOs to own a concise one-to-two-page document outlining the strategy and objectives. Examples illustrate how such a document can address specific risks faced by businesses and the desired accounting outcomes. The chapter highlights the crucial need for hedge eligibility criteria to be met throughout the hedge relationship. It emphasises the importance of proper documentation and discusses eligible hedging instruments and common pitfalls to avoid when selecting hedging products. By providing an overview of hedge accounting, its strategies, and eligibility requirements, this chapter sets the stage for readers to delve deeper into the complexities of hedge accounting practices, enabling them to make informed decisions to mitigate financial risks effectively.

Hedge Accounting Overview

Below are some of the basic principles of hedge accounting, the benefits of applying hedge accounting and a description of the different types of hedges. To remove any room for misinterpretation, I have also defined the different types of hedge relationships.

The overarching principle of IFRS 9 - Hedge Accounting is to show the risk management activities in the financial accounts, allowing companies to offset gains or losses from financial instruments used to manage risks, such as foreign exchange rate fluctuations, commodity price movements or interest rate changes.

Hedge accounting is complex and requires careful documentation and analysis, but it will provide a more accurate representation of your company's financial position and performance if done correctly. It involves identifying the specific risk that a company wants to manage and designating a corresponding financial instrument as a hedge against that risk. The company must then document the relationship between the hedge and the risk being managed and track the effectiveness of the hedge over time. Depending on the level of effectiveness measured, there are different accounting treatments. (This is covered in more detail in later chapters.)

There are three types of hedge relationships, namely:

1. Cash Flow Hedge

2. Fair Value Hedge

3. Net Investment Hedge

Cash Flow Hedge

Cash flow hedge is the most common type of hedge relationship I see in practice, as it provides the most beneficial accounting treatment. This type of hedge is used to manage the risk of cash flow variability that arises from changes in the fair value of a company's assets, liabilities, or forecasted transactions. A company uses a financial instrument, such as a forward contract or an interest rate swap, to offset changes in the value of a specific cash flow that is expected to occur. This cash flow can be related to a transaction that has already been entered into or a forecasted transaction that is likely to occur in the future. Examples of cash flow hedges are discussed further in the next chapter.

Why are cash flow hedges the most common?

Simply put, the cash flow hedge of a forecast transaction can generate the most beneficial accountant treatment. Unlike foreign currency Accounts Receivable (A/R) and Accounts Payable (A/P), which are already booked in the general ledger and adjusted every month, a foreign currency forecast will not produce mirroring journal entries to offset the amounts from the foreign FX contract. This creates detrimental fluctuations in reporting, which can sometimes put a CFO off hedging at all!

The CFO may think they are doing the smart thing by hedging, but then they are presented with a significant hedge revaluation problem. However, by applying hedge accounting and designating the hedge as a cash flow hedge, unrealised gains or losses on the foreign exchange contracts can be parked into the cash flow hedge reserve, significantly altering your financial statements and reducing volatility in profit or loss. (A more detailed case study on this is available in Chapter 7).

Fair Value Hedge

This type of hedge is used to manage the risk of changes in the fair value of a company's assets, liabilities, or other financial instruments. The hedging instrument should have a fair value highly correlated with the fair value of the underlying transaction being hedged. For example, if a company has fixed-rate debt and wants to hedge the exposure to changes in fair value because of changes in market interest rates.

Net Investment Hedge

This type of hedge is used to manage the foreign exchange risk of changes in the value of a company's investments in foreign subsidiaries due to fluctuations in exchange rates. A company uses a financial instrument, such as a forward contract or an option, to offset the changes in the value of its net investment in a foreign operation. Therefore, it is the translation of net assets from a foreign operation into the group's functional currency that is the designated hedged risk. All the gains or losses on the hedges are quarantined with equity until the disposal of the subsidiary.

Along with some of the benefits of hedge accounting, this section has explained the main principle under IFRS 9 and introduces the three types of hedge relationships. Selecting the correct type of hedge designation is paramount.

Hedge Eligibility Criteria

Hedge accounting is only allowable subject to meeting prescribed conditions at the inception of the hedge relationship and throughout. Importantly, should the criteria not be met throughout the hedge relationship, a company can risk the hedge accounting program being pulled by the auditor. This unwanted outcome can result in significant gains or losses reported in profit or loss.

IFRS 9 provides the essential requirements for companies to qualify for hedge accounting, and they include the following:

1. The hedging relationship should be appropriately documented with prescribed areas.

2. The hedging instrument and hedge item need to be eligible.

3. The hedge needs to be effective.

Every single hedge must be documented with a formal document. The key areas on this document or form should include the following:

- The nature of the risk and type of hedge.

- An outline of the risk management strategy and objectives.

- A description of the hedged item and how this impacts profit or loss.

- Any sources or ineffectiveness and how this will be assessed.

- A description of how hedge ineffectiveness will be measured.

Hedge Relationship Documentation is discussed in more detail in Chapter 3.

What is eligible and ineligible?

From a hedging instrument perspective, most of my clients want to hedge with financial derivatives that do qualify for hedge accounting. Eligible products include FX Forward contacts, Vanilla FX Options, Commodity Futures, Interest Rate Swaps, and Interest Rate Options. Things get tricky when clients are proposed certain hedging products by their banking counterpart or treasury advisor. The rule of thumb here is that the more exotic the option or technical the hedge, the closer attention and analysis you should take to ensure it qualifies for hedge accounting. If you don't understand the hedging outcomes and the trigger events yourself, source an independent specialist who does.

I often see new clients have been ill-advised and remain exposed to the risks they thought they were hedging against. Most traders I've worked with are very professional, but at the end of the day, the executing partners are not independent and are compensated based on the volume of trading they do, and the larger the bank spreads, the more they get paid. As a CFO, it's about being as informed as possible so you can keep them honest.

Only hedging derivatives measured at fair value through profit or loss can qualify for hedge accounting treatment. The main requirement of the hedged item is to display the same risk components or characteristics as the hedging instrument so that they will offset each other.

Which hedging instruments qualify?

At first glance, some non-vanilla hedge relationships might only appear to meet some of the criteria. It is always worth getting a second opinion on the hedge relationships that fall into this category, as there may be another way to present the argument that can make a difference to the outcome. We investigate an example or two of this later in this book. Some of the more non-vanilla hedging instruments are discussed below:

Hedging Instrument	Description	Eligible Y/N
Zero Cost Collar Option	These contracts are constructed with a combination of a Call and Put option, both with the same notional amount. So long as no net premium is received and the notional on the sold option is at least equal in size to the purchased option, then they can be designated as a hedging instrument.	Yes
Net Written Option	These options do not qualify as hedging instruments. A net-written option is when the sold option has a greater notional than the purchased option.	No
Deal-Contingent Hedge	These types of hedges are less straightforward and must be examined on a case-by-case basis. As the name suggests, the risk being hedged is dependent on the occurrence of a future event, and therefore, the hedge will contain a knock-out option to protect the buyer of the option should the event not occur. The probability of the deal will need to be considered carefully, and how effective the hedge will be from a hedge effectiveness perspective before a deal-contingent hedge is designated for hedge accounting.	Possible
Participating Forward Option	If the company is buying the option, then these structures can qualify for hedge accounting.	Yes
Interest Rate Swap with a Floor	If the debt facility has an interest rate floor, meaning the bank does not pay interest to the client if the rate goes negative, then to improve hedge effectiveness the hedge should also have a floor, which is effectively a bought option. If the client is receiving floating interest, then if interest rates drop to less than 0% then the client would not be required to receive negative interest i.e. pay interest to the bank. Therefore, as long as the floor is mirrored in the hedging instrument and the hedged item then this will qualify for hedge accounting treatment. Some organisations might believe due to market conditions that the chances are interest rates dropping to 0% over the term of the hedge are very slim and decide to save on the cost of the option. This approach might be good from a cash flow perspective as you save in the premium paid for the bought option, however it would lead to more hedge ineffectiveness and profit or loss volatility.	Yes
Knock In / Knock Out Options	For some hedging strategies, there can be a cost advantage to include knock-in or knock-out components to the hedge. This will increase hedge ineffectiveness should the knock-in or knock-out features not be also present in the hedged item, which is likely the case.	Possible but expect PnL volatility

It's important to consider that just because a hedging instrument is ineligible for hedge accounting, it might still be something the organisation decides to use. Some companies might not be as interested in the accounting result and focus on the cash flow impact, or the estimates of fair value movements into profit or loss might not be material enough to worry about.

Accounting versus cash – which wins?

The immediate response is usually 'Cash is King', but protecting the Earnings Before Interest, Tax, Depreciation, and Amortisation (EBITDA) is vital for some organisations. It can drive some of the strategies in which hedging products can be used based on their eligibility for hedge accounting. This is why it is essential that everyone is on the same page and that the High-Level Strategy document is circulated and acknowledged by all the main stakeholders.

I'm aware of situations when hedging products that don't qualify for hedge accounting but make perfect sense from the protection of cash flow have been executed by the traders or treasury team, only to have then it be reversed or closed out once the accounting team or CFO has realised the Market-To-Market (MTM) must be fair value through the profit and loss account (FVTPL) for those products. One way to avoid this oversight is to have a clear policy and a well-communicated strategy across the relevant stakeholders.

Hedged items (underlying exposures)

The main requirement of the hedged item is that it displays the same risk components or characteristics as the hedging instrument so that they will offset each other consistently and effectively over the term of the hedge relationship. The common hedged items in foreign exchange are A/R, A/P and CoGS, or an investment in an offshore subsidiary. In commodity hedging, clients will generally be hedging against the future input price of gold, iron ore, or coal, for example. Financing facilities and securitising interest-generating assets are common interest-rate exposures that businesses look to hedge. These are all fine from an eligibility perspective as long as the hedge documentation is prescriptive.

Not all types of risk exposures are eligible for hedge accounting. The hedged item needs to be reliably measured, and in the case of a forecast exposure, it must be highly probable. A few hedge item examples that fall foul of the standard are outlined below:

Intercompany transactions

With a few exceptions, only hedged items that have a contractual agreement with an external party to the reporting entity are eligible hedged items.

Hedging own equity

Designating risks associated with an organisation's equity share-based payments does not qualify for hedge accounting. This is because items such as forecast dividend payments will not impact profit or loss; these distributions are deducted directly from equity.

The hedge is effective

For this to hold, the first point of call is to check all the critical terms of the hedged item and the hedging instrument. Do they match? Using a Matched Terms Checklist is an excellent way to tick off all the key terms, which brings me to my first free resource, which you can download from the link below.

Hedge effectiveness testing is covered in more detail in Chapter 5.

DOWNLOADABLE RESOURCE #1

The objective of carrying out a matched terms test it to demonstrate that relevant stakeholders have reviewed all the critical aspects of the hedge item and hedging instrument to ascertain whether there is any scope for hedge ineffectiveness. Any variations in the matched terms will impact hedge effectiveness. Should all key terms match, then the hedge can be expected to be highly effective.

Download here:

https://www.hedgeeffective.com/hedge-accounting/resources

Strategy and Objectives

In this section, I'll review the big-picture information that should be clear from the beginning of any hedging accounting program. Embarking on a hedge accounting strategy must be articulated and understood by the finance and accounting teams, the treasury teams and the relevant board or sub-committee. If hedge accounting is entirely new to you and your organisation, then you might look at outsourcing the design of the strategy and even some of the implementation to a third-party specialist; however, this doesn't mean you shouldn't understand the high-level approach presented. Ultimately, the CFO is responsible for the outcomes of the agreed strategy.

This section will also cover the link between the treasury risk management activities undertaken and how they interlink with the hedge accounting treatment. There can be situations when decisions are made without due consideration for the accounting outcome, aligned to achieving the business objectives, which is the primary key performance indicator of any hedging program.

The best practice is to prepare a position paper outlining the hedge accounting strategy and objectives, which should be circulated and acknowledged by all the critical stakeholders in the organisation. This can be prepared by the CFO, a team member, or an outsourced specialist, but as the CFO, you must own the document.

The key areas to cover would include:

Background

Summarise the type of risk(s) the business is exposed to and the risk management activities intended to mitigate these risks (s). Some examples might be:

Exposure	Description	Objectives
FX Risk for an Importer	An importer of goods is concerned about the impact of foreign exchange risk on the underlying gross profit margins. Adverse movements in foreign exchange rates will increase the AUD equivalent of their foreign currency CoGS. Due to their commoditised product (i.e. white t-shirt sold in Target that has a low price elasticity of demand), they are not in a position to pass on any of the foreign exchange risks to the consumer, as the price would become uncompetitive.	The cost of goods sold is purchased offshore, and the gross margins and profitability will be unreliable unless they are hedged. The business decides to proactively manage this risk by entering into FX Forward contracts (FECs) against the forecasted purchases to lock in future rates, providing certainty of cash flows for the business.
Interest Rate Risk on Variable Debt	A capital-intensive business requires a significant amount of debt to fund its operations. The financiers provide the debt at a floating rate, and the business is concerned by the future interest rate environment and likely increases in interest costs. There is also an obligation to hedge a proportion of the financing facility to ensure the business stays above the desired level of interest cover, i.e., financial covenant.	Management decides to manage this risk by entering into an interest rate swap (IRS) with a bank that swaps the floating interest to a fixed amount, providing certainty of cash flows to the business.

FX Risk of Fund NAV & Income Returns	A fund manager is providing investment opportunities to investors in global assets. They are concerned that the fund's performance could be negatively impacted by adverse movements in foreign exchange risks and, therefore, mitigate this risk with a hedged class of units in the fund for those investors who don't want to be exposed to FX risk.	The fund manager must also consider the tax impact of your risk management activities so that investors' distributions are not impacted by gains or losses on the hedging. The fund undertakes a currency overly mandate to hedge the FX risk on the NAV and income of the fund that meets the hedge accounting criteria. The Tax Of Financial Arrangements (TOFA) hedging election is also obtained.
Commodity Price Risk	A coffee manufacturer wants to hedge the future costs of coffee to protect margin. They are contracted to purchase coffee from their supplier based on the 'Coffee ICE Futures' plus a delivery fee in 12 months.	The manufacturer enters into a hedge of the Coffee ICE Futures price to hedge the variability in coffee in 12 months, providing certainty of cash flows.

Hedge accounting assessment

This section should link to the standard eligibility criteria and assess whether the hedges will qualify.

Accounting mechanics

Provides the high-level accounting impact desired, including the GL Accounts impacted and the journals required.

DOWNLOADABLE RESOURCE #2

This Hedge Accounting Strategy document represents a concise two-page document outlining the strategy and objectives of the hedging program. The main sections include the background and level of exposures the business faces, the risk management activities required to mitigate these risks, how hedge accounting will be achieved, and the desired accounting outcomes.

Download here:

https://www.hedgeeffective.com/hedge-accounting/resources

Summary

In Chapter 1, I set the stage for our exploration of hedge accounting. I began by laying out the eligibility criteria for this complex accounting treatment. I delved into the core principles, including gain and loss offsetting within financial instruments designed to manage financial risks. I also introduced you to the three types of hedge relationships: cash flow, fair value, and net investment hedges.

There is a critical need to document high-level strategies in hedge accounting, ensuring clear articulation and comprehension among stakeholders. While outsourcing the strategy's design is an option, CFOs must grasp the approach. I recommended creating a concise document outlining the hedge accounting strategy and objectives, with risk examples and mitigation strategies. Accounting and cash flow objectives must be aligned, and eligibility criteria for hedge accounting should be outlined, highlighting the importance of documenting hedge relationships and distinguishing eligible and ineligible hedging instruments.

By the end of this chapter, you should feel well-equipped to make informed decisions and understand the qualifications for hedge accounting, thus minimising potential risks in your financial strategies.

Chapter 1 — Key Takeaways

- Hedge accounting should provide a more accurate representation of your company's financial position and performance when managing financial market risks with derivatives.
- To qualify for hedge accounting, key criteria must be achieved. Not all hedging instruments are eligible.
- The hedge accounting strategy

Chapter 2:
Effective Policy Document

Introduction

When embarking on a hedge accounting program, having an adequate policy document is crucial for organisations of all sizes. While larger or listed entities may have a mandatory requirement for a formal policy, private or smaller businesses can benefit from documenting their approach to hedge accounting and derivative management. This chapter highlights the significance of a Derivative and Hedge Accounting Policy (DHAP) in providing governance, control, and structure. The DHAP serves as a guide for applying hedge accounting under International Financial Reporting Standards (IFRS), focusing on IFRS 9 — Financial Instruments. It outlines accounting policies, procedures, and relevant accounting guidance while not addressing economic risk management hedging issues or specific hedging strategies. The chapter also introduces the concept of an Audit Pack, a concise document summarising vital information for the audit team. The pack assists in streamlining the audit process, saving time, and reducing the number of questions asked.

In summary, an effective policy document, such as the DHAP, plays a vital role in the success of a hedge accounting program. It strengthens governance, reduces errors, aids staff development, and streamlines the audit process. The following sections of this chapter will delve into the key components of a DHAP, outlining its contents and the benefits they offer.

Why have a Derivative & Hedge Accounting Policy?

A formal hedge accounting policy is mandatory in some organisations, significantly larger or listed entities. There will be a strict protocol for any adjustments made to the policy, which would include dates the changes are made and by whom. Even for private or smaller businesses, there are benefits of taking the time to document your policy on hedge accounting and the accounting for derivatives.

Typically, a Derivative and Hedge Accounting Policy (DHAP) is written from the perspective of hedges and hedged items that exist at a consolidated level. However, this is not meant to preclude the application of hedge accounting for inter-company risks, if appropriate. Inter-company hedge accounting transactions would be eliminated for consolidated reporting, with other inter-company activity.

A Derivative and Hedge Accounting Policy will govern the application of derivative and hedge accounting under IFRS, particularly concerning hedge accounting activities. The

DHAP is not to be confused with the company's Treasury Risk Management Policy. The intention is not to address economic risk management hedging issues or the hedging strategies undertaken. Instead, to discuss the application of IFRS 9. The policy should also document accounting policies and procedures for derivative and hedge accounting activities. GAAP and other relevant accounting guidance should also be addressed.

The main benefits of having a formal policy document centre around applying governance and control. Suppose specific policies and procedures are in black and white and part of your job description to follow them. This will create more structure and less scope for errors and mistakes, which could become significant when dealing with financial derivatives. Another important reason for having a policy is staff development onboarding and training.

Personal Anecdote

Many years ago, one of my first hedge accounting customers was implementing a hedge accounting program for the first time. Nobody in the treasury operations team had any hedge accounting experience. The organisation was a mid to large business with foreign exchange exposures in multiple currencies, which it wanted to manage proactively. Fortunately, the CFO was very experienced, understood best-practice processes, and instructed me to create a DHAP to govern the new approach to managing foreign exchange risk. The CFO was on the Audit and Risk Committee, a sub-committee to the board, and the DHAP was tabled for the next meeting for scrutiny and formal approval. The Treasury Operations Team was then able to reference the DHAP when seeking clarification, especially in the early stages of the program, before they built up confidence and awareness of the regular process. This example highlights the benefit of a DHAP to ensure all stakeholders are across the strategy.

What's Contained Within A DHAP?

I will now highlight the key components of an effective DHAP and why they are essential.

Roles and responsibilities/delegations of authority

The roles and responsibilities of the main stakeholders should be clearly laid out within the policy. Some examples would be:

- The CFO is typically responsible for the company-wide adherence to IFRS 9.

- The CFO should implement consistent accounting policies and procedures, which govern and guide all derivative accounting activities.

- Changes to the DHAP are to be approved by the CFO with notice provided to the Board or sub-committee, i.e. the Audit & Risk Committee.

- Hedge accounting documentation (including designations, de-designations, and re-designations) should be signed off by any two of the approved Derivative Authorised Signatories.

Additional authorisation and guidelines could be provided in the Treasury Risk Management Policy and Schedule of Delegated Authority.

IFRS 9 philosophy

The DHAP should be developed to provide a framework and philosophy for applying IFRS 9 at the group level, including all entities within the group engaging in derivative and hedging activities.

Description of the derivatives and hedging activities

Authorisation of the company to use derivative instruments to manage its exposure to changes to interest rates and to manage the movements in foreign exchange rates or commodity prices. For example, utilising interest rate swaps to pay fixed and receive floating rates, or vice versa. The use of these instruments might be driven by factors such as a target fixed versus floating debt position or management's preference based on the economic outlook. For global businesses with foreign operations, there is exposure to foreign exchange rates and authority to hedge these using a variety of financial instruments. Vitally, there should be a statement that using treasury-related derivatives is limited to non-speculative transactions within any hedge accounting policy.

Designation, documentation, and authorisation requirements for hedge accounting

Another crucial section of the DHAP is the Hedge Relationship Documentation requirements. This is covered in more detail in Chapter 3.

Useful Appendices to the DHAP include:

- Hedge Relationship Documentation form example

- Effectiveness test calculation example

- Journal entries example

In this section, we discussed the key contents of a DHAP, which is crucial for managing risk exposure. It's essential to clarify the roles and responsibilities of relevant stakeholders and the appropriate use of derivative instruments. The CFO ensures that the company adheres to IFRS 9 and implements consistent accounting policies and procedures. Any changes made to the DHAP must follow the prescribed protocol to safeguard the organisation. The DHAP provides a framework and philosophy for applying IFRS 9.

The Audit Pack

I will explain why I produce an Audit Pack, who the intended recipient is, and why they will find it helpful. Generating this document also benefits the company by streamlining the audit process, reducing the time spent and reducing the number of hedge accounting-related questions asked.

The Audit Pack is a short document produced for the audit team's benefit and is particularly useful when implementing or changing a hedge accounting program. The document should summarise the essential information from the hedge relationship documentation forms and the DHAP and provide the auditor with a clear overview of the program. This should get the audit team up to speed and reduce the time they need to sit with your team members.

I typically include sections on the following areas:

- Executive Summary — This consists of the strategy and objectives.

- Accounting Outcomes — a summary of how the gains and losses will impact profit or loss and the accounting optics in the financial statements.

- Process mapping schematic (example in Figure 1 below)

- Example of the hedge relationship documentation

Providing this information and detail is well received by my audit teams, who often have different personnel on the team from one year to the next. The last thing you want as a CFO is to have to repeat yourself or provide walk-throughs on the process each year. This document is an excellent first port of call to reduce the number of questions asked.

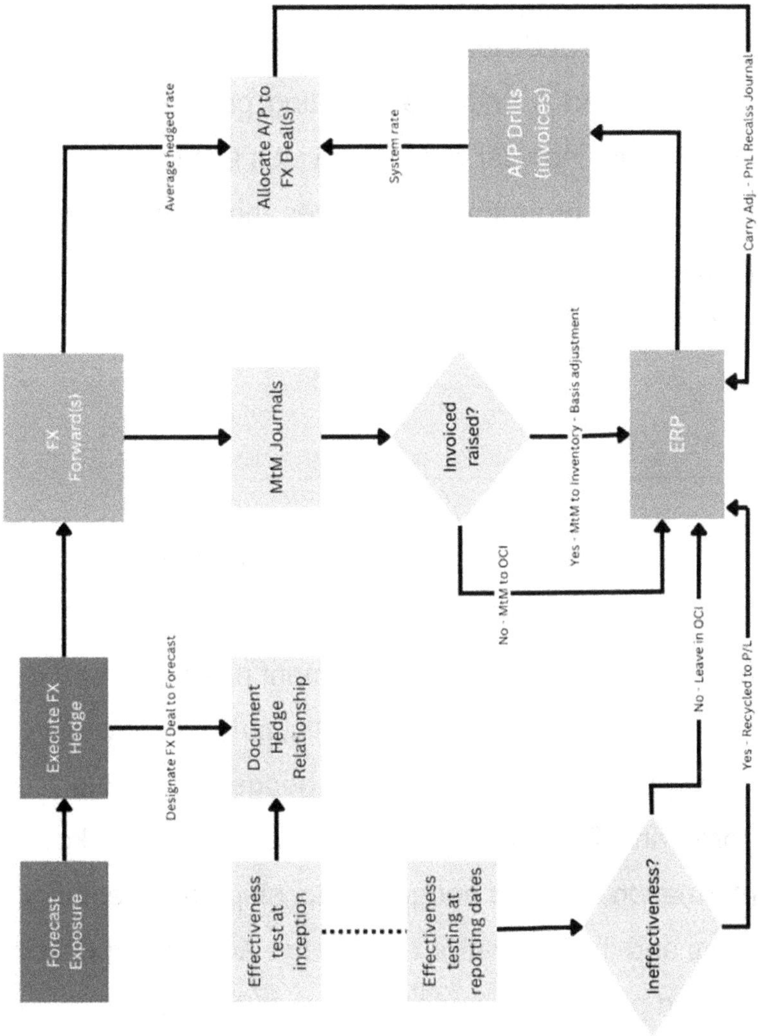

Figure 1: Process Mapping Schematic Example

You should now understand the key components of the Audit Pack, a short document summarising key information from hedge relationship documentation forms and the DHAP. It is produced for the audit team's benefit, mainly when a company has implemented a hedge accounting program for the first time during the financial year. It provides auditors with a clear overview of the program and reduces the need for repeated explanations or walkthroughs; this saves everyone time and energy, including the CFO.

DOWNLOADABLE RESOURCE #3

The Audit Pack is a short document produced for the audit team's benefit and is particularly useful when implementing or changing a hedge accounting program. The document should summarise the key information from the hedge relationship documentation forms and the Derivative and Hedge Accounting Policy and provide the auditor a clear overview of the program.

Download here:

https://www.hedgeeffective.com/hedge-accounting/resources

Summary

An effective policy document is crucial for organisations embarking on a hedge accounting program. While larger or listed entities may be required to have a formal policy, even smaller businesses can benefit from documenting their policy on hedge accounting and derivatives.

The DHAP governs the application of derivative and hedge accounting under IFRS and provides guidelines for accounting policies and procedures. The main advantages of a formal policy document include establishing governance and control, reducing errors and mistakes, and facilitating staff development and training.

The DHAP outlines roles and responsibilities, addresses IFRS 9 requirements, describes derivatives and hedging activities, and specifies designation and documentation requirements. Additionally, creating an Audit Pack will streamline the audit process and provide auditors with a clear overview of the program, reducing the need for repeated explanations and saving time for all stakeholders involved.

Chapter 2 — Key Takeaways

- The DHAP governs and controls the application of hedge accounting for the organisation.
- An Audit Pack assists in streamlining the audit process and is especially useful for newly implemented hedge accounting programs.

Part Two

Part two examines elements 3 to 6 of the HEDGEHOG method. The previous section focused on the initial strategy, setting up and getting ready to implement your hedge accounting program. This section is about practical implementation and goes deep into the fundamental requirements of running a hedge accounting program: the hedge relationship documentation, effectiveness testing, disclosure requirements and accounting journal entries.

Overlooking the importance of accurately documenting the relationship between hedging instruments and hedged items is something the CFO needs to avoid at all costs. The aim is to have precise and accurate entries into the general ledger, minimising errors and inaccuracies in hedge accounting reporting. Therefore, rigorous testing of the hedge relationships should be conducted. Inadequate or improper effectiveness testing may result in incorrect assessments of hedge effectiveness, which can lead to significant profit or loss volatility down the track. The production of transparent disclosures in financial statements is also essential. Failing to provide comprehensive disclosures related to hedge accounting activities in financial statements could present a poor and inaccurate view of the company, which is not 'true and fair'.

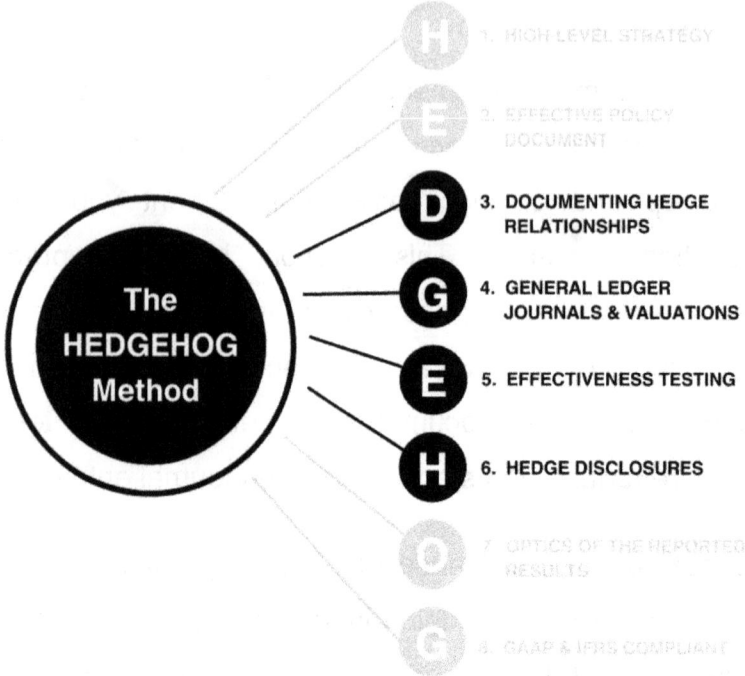

H 1. HIGH-LEVEL STRATEGY

E 2. EFFECTIVE POLICY DOCUMENT

D 3. DOCUMENTING HEDGE RELATIONSHIPS

G 4. GENERAL LEDGER JOURNALS & VALUATIONS

E 5. EFFECTIVENESS TESTING

H 6. HEDGE DISCLOSURES

O 7. OPTICS OF THE REPORTED RESULTS

G 8. GAAP & IFRS COMPLIANT

The HEDGEHOG Method

Chapter 3:
Documenting the Hedge Relationship

Introduction

This chapter will delve into the significance of preparing hedge relationship documentation. We will also discuss what information should be included in the forms. This chapter builds upon the concepts introduced in the previous two chapters. Specifically, some strategy and policy documentation information can be reused in the individual hedge forms. Unfortunately, there are many instances where mistakes are made in the documentation. Worse, sometimes the process and theory outlined in the documentation isn't carried out in practice, or the documentation needs to be prepared. This section will shed light on the common problem areas seen in practice. By doing so, CFOs can ensure that their teams are following the requirements of IFRS 9.

What Areas Should Be Included?

Documenting the hedge relationship is non-negotiable and is one of the criteria mentioned in IFRS 9 that you must meet to qualify for hedge accounting treatment. If you undertake many hedges in a month, these requirements can be cumbersome and an administrative burden unless you have a well-oiled operation. With appropriate hedge relationship documentation in place, hedge accounting can be undertaken. Here are the main sections and a description of the requirements:

Hedge Form Component	Description
Nature of the risk being hedged	Specify here the risk being hedged. Are there risks associated with variations in future cash flows or fair value movements? Ideally, you will already have the High-level Strategy document prepared and can simply pull the description of the risk from this document. Two or three sentences describing the nature of the risk and underlying exposure is enough.
Policy declaration	This is nice to have and isn't mandatory. However, if there is another treasury policy that speaks to hedging, such as a treasury risk management policy and/or the DHAP, then it's good practice to reference those here.

Risk management strategy	At the highest level, a sentence or two explaining the overarching risk management strategy and why this is important to the company.
Hedge type	Confirmation of the type of hedge: Is it a cash flow hedge, fair value hedge or net investment hedge?
Date of designation and review and sign-off dates	These dates are typically the same day, usually the date of execution.
Hedging instrument details	Include here as much information on the financial derivative being used. Must haves include the type of product used, the notional amount, the effective and maturity dates, counterparties to the trade, and the percentage of the notional being hedged. Nice to haves are the Day 1 MTM on the hedge in dollar terms and the cash flows to be received and paid at maturity.

Hedged item details	Describe the nature of the underlying exposure and how this will impact profit or loss. Then, record similar to the hedging instrument, namely the notional amount, the effective and maturity dates, counterparties and the percentage of the notional being hedged. If the exposure is a group of hedged items that share the same underlying risk, then this should be specified in this section.
Hedge effectiveness assessment	Information needs to be provided as to the existence of an economic relationship at inception, which you would reasonably expect the hedge to be highly effective; for example, the underlying risk is the same; therefore, the changes in fair value are expected to offset.
Effect of changes in credit risk	The company needs to declare if it will monitor the impact of changes to the counterparty's credit risk. This is an area most organisations won't know how to do unless they have an experienced treasury team. A separate section has been added later in this chapter and Chapter 4 to elaborate further on the requirements.

Quantification of hedge ineffectiveness	Description of the methodology to be used to measure the ineffectiveness and how this will be recorded in profit or loss. Again, this is an area most organisations won't know how to do unless they have an experienced treasury team. A separate section has been added later in this chapter to elaborate further on the requirements.
Expected sources of hedge ineffectiveness	Provide an overview of where you believe there will be some ineffectiveness present. Some common sources include credit risk, variations in timings of cash flows, currency basis risk and designation of off-market hedging instruments, i.e., Day one MTM. A separate section has been added later in this chapter to elaborate further on the requirements.
Testing frequency	Document when you will perform the testing. The absolute minimum you should do this is at reporting dates, but you should also do this on an ad-hoc basis if any events occur that could impact hedge ineffectiveness.

Following this comprehensive layout will ensure professional documentation and adherence to hedge accounting standards. The downloadable template below will help you create your Hedge Relationship Form.

DOWNLOADABLE RESOURCE #4

Documenting the hedge relationship is a non-negotiable and is one of the specified criteria mentioned in IFRS 9 you must meet, to be able to qualify for hedge accounting treatment. This template provides the standard method for presenting the Hedge Relationship Form.

Download here:

https://www.hedgeeffective.com/hedge-accounting/resources

Common Mistakes

This section will highlight some common oversights when preparing hedge relationship documentation. Mistakes at this stage can create unwanted and severe consequences if not corrected before the audit and once the books are closed. If you have never produced a hedge relationship form before, seek professional assistance to ensure you don't make some of the mistakes highlighted below.

The hedge relationship form is not prepared

What happens if you forget to document the hedge? This depends on when this oversight has been picked up and by whom. I have seen hedge documentation prepared late, and this sometimes gets through if you are still within the same reporting period and before an auditor has picked it up. When an auditor cannot locate the hedge documentation for a specific hedge, they typically accept a missing form with no further action if it seems to be a simple oversight and there's evidence of documentation for other trades tied to the same risk. This is especially true if the risk being hedged is a long-standing exposure that the company has been hedge accounting for a while. However, suppose this is a new risk being hedged, and there's no evidence of this being designated in a hedge relationship. In that case, they will unlikely allow you to obtain the beneficial hedge accounting treatment.

From their perspective, due to the hedging instruments being in a loss position at year-end, the company has since decided they don't want the profit or loss account to be adversely impacted and have now cherry-picked this contract for hedge accounting purposes, which is akin to manipulating the financial results by retrospectively electing to document the hedge in a hedge relationship.

The hedge relationship form doesn't reflect reality

As the personal anecdote below discusses further, a common oversight is to correctly prepare the hedge relationship form under IFRS 9 on paper but be unable to apply the theory in practice. The practical elements of a hedge accounting program can be delegated to team members, but the CFO or Financial Controller should ensure the accounting policy is carried through. Sometimes, there is a breakdown in communication and reporting lines, with a lack of sign-offs allowing things to slip through the cracks.

Personal Anecdote

A CFO engaged me to review their hedge accounting documentation and policy. The business supplied credit to retail customers for items such as cars and household appliances. They were exposed to movements in interest rates as they borrowed money at variable rates. On reviewing the hedge documentation, everything looked in compliance and above board. However, what was happening in practice didn't align with the documentation's declarations, especially in the effectiveness testing approach or lack thereof. Fortunately, this was picked up before the audit, and the hedging program was still in its infancy, so the accounting was corrected with no harm done. The corrections involved recognising some hedge ineffectiveness, resulting in a minor adjustment of a few hundred thousand dollars to profit or loss to ensure compliance. However, this issue could have become more significant in a year or two if the CFO hadn't proactively investigated.

How To Monitor The Effect Of Changes To Credit Risk

A requirement of IFRS 9 when preparing the hedge relationship form is for the reporting entity to declare how they will assess the effect of changes in credit risk on the hedge relationship. The reporting entity needs to provide a short statement acknowledging whether there is credit risk associated with the hedge relationship based on the credit risk of both the company and the counterparty, how the company will monitor the credit risk, and how they can measure the significance of changes in the credit risk by performing relevant analysis, such as the Credit Valuation Adjustment (CVA) and Debit Valuation Adjustment (DVA) estimates. The credit risk should be assessed at the hedge's inception and then re-assessed at reporting dates, especially when there is a significant change to either party's circumstances.

In many hedge relationships, the reporting entity states that they expect the changes in credit risk to be minimal. Suppose the company believes the impact of credit risk will make the offset between the hedged item and the hedging instrument ineffective and dominate the economic relationship between the two. In that case, they should undertake further quantitative analysis at inception and ongoing. For more information on Credit Risk, check out Chapter 4.

Failure to identify sources of ineffectiveness

When preparing your hedge relationship documentation, the possible sources of hedge ineffectiveness should be understood and documented. Some hedge relationships will have more sources than others, but failing to disclose them at inception signals that the hedge accounting program is unlikely to be accurate in practice. It's important to document at the hedge's inception what these sources could be and how significant they are likely to be, as this may influence the type of ineffectiveness testing required.

Strategy to monitor hedge ineffectiveness

At inception, it should be evident within the documentation how the reporting entity intends to measure ineffectiveness and how this transpires into the accounting entries. Errors occur when the reporting entity believes the hedge to be 100% effective. The reporting entity must assert that they can match the Key Terms and that an economic relationship exists between the hedging instrument and the underlying hedged item; we call this a qualitative assessment. In practice, the most common oversight to make is that the Day 1 fair value of the hedge instrument is zero. If Key Terms don't match, and it's expected this may impact the offset in gains or losses on the hedging instrument versus the hedged item, then further quantitative testing is needed. The reporting entity should disclose how they will measure, track and account for hedge ineffectiveness in the hedge relationship documentation. As we will cover in Chapter 5 on Effectiveness Testing, this is a technical area that generally requires sophisticated systems to undertake. This can lead to inconsistencies in the hedge form and what's posted in the GL.

Streamlining the Process

There is, of course, an administrative burden to preparing hedge relationship documentation. Creating these forms without a Treasury Management System (TMS) or similar tools can be time-consuming. One workaround is to develop a semi-automatic process where only certain sections of the forms change based on individual hedging amounts while the majority remains static. Another option is to prepare the forms in bulk at monthly intervals or use a single form linked to a schedule of related hedging instruments. However, I don't recommend the latter approach; a one-to-one form-to-instrument ratio is preferable.

Some organisations may opt to prepare something other than the Hedge Relationship Form for every hedge and instead wait until the reporting period to prepare forms for all open hedges at the reporting date. While some auditors may allow this, it doesn't strictly align with the standard's intent, and consequences of non-compliance may result.

The resource link below will take you to a downloadable Hedge Relationship Form containing dynamic and static data sections.

DOWNLOADABLE RESOURCE #5

Documenting the hedge relationship is a non-negotiable and is one of the specified criteria mentioned in IFRS 9 you must meet, to be able to qualify for hedge accounting treatment. This link provides an example of how to semi-automate the production of the Hedge Relationship Form efficiently by using dynamic fields to populate the form quickly.

Download here:

https://www.hedgeeffective.com/hedge-accounting/resources

Summary

In this chapter, I highlighted the critical components of a Hedge Relationship Form and emphasised the importance of accurate and comprehensive documentation for successful hedge accounting practices. Precise documentation is pivotal in ensuring compliance and effective hedge accounting.

To help avoid common mistakes, I provided guidance on preparing the hedge relationship form and aligning it with actual practices. I also stressed the significance of monitoring changes in credit risk, quantifying hedge ineffectiveness, and identifying expected sources of ineffectiveness.

Furthermore, I discussed the administrative challenges associated with these forms and offered practical tips and workarounds to enhance efficiency. These included implementing semi-automatic processes, utilising static and dynamic sections within the documentation, and considering options like bulk preparation or a single-form approach. These approaches aimed to streamline the documentation process and improve overall efficiency.

Chapter 3 – Key Takeaways

- Producing hedge relationship documentation is a necessary requirement for every hedge.
- Streamline the production of hedge relationship documentation with dynamic fields and a systemised approach.
- Failure to heed some of the common pitfalls in hedge relationship documentation can result in serious repercussions later, resulting in significant volatility to profit or loss.

Chapter 4:
General Ledger Journals & Valuations

Introduction

This chapter focuses on the entries that hit the general ledger, sometimes called the ERP (Enterprise Resource Planning). The typical accounting entries to record are the fair values of the derivative contracts and the entries relating to the contracts' gains or losses, whether these are reclassification journals or cost-basis adjustments. Financial derivatives are measured at fair value under IFRS 13. This chapter will examine the fair value calculations for common hedging instruments and the debits and credits in the general ledger. We also cover the effects of credit risk on the derivative fair values and how this should be recorded. These are called Credit Valuation Adjustments (CVA) and Debit Valuations Adjustments (DVA).

Fair Value Basics

Understanding the concepts around fair value measurement is one of the fundamentals in hedge accounting, as the fair value of a financial derivative is where most hedge accounting entries originate. Here, we will cover the classification and measurement requirements for financial derivatives and some of the IFRS 13 framework, which feeds into IFRS 9 and provides a definition of fair value.

IFRS 9 states that all derivatives are accounted for on the balance sheet at fair value. Under IFRS 13, a fair value is the price received to sell an asset or the amount paid to settle a liability between market participants. The fair value should reflect current market conditions.

Valuations can be derived under three main methods according to IFRS 13, namely:

1. The Market Method

2. The Cost Method

3. The Income Method

It's the income approach used for financial derivatives. The income approach is a valuation technique that converts future cash flows into a present-day value. A good example is the fair value of an interest rate swap, discussed later in this chapter. The present-day value is a measurement technique that uses a discount rate and should include the expected future cash flows and adjustments for credit risk.

Why do some valuations from different providers differ?

It is common to receive two separate valuations for the same derivative at the reporting date but with a variation in the measured fair value. This is due to the inputs used to measure the fair value taken at different times of the day, for example, an EOD close rate in APAC versus an End-Of-Day (EOD) close rate in New York—various providers source rates from multiple market data vendors. Therefore, a bank will apply its own interest rate curve, which would differ from another bank or the interest curve used by a third-party treasury management system. Any material differences due to market data timing differences should be demonstrable upon investigation. A bank will also adjust its valuation for its own credit risk reporting requirements, so valuations are shown net of credit adjustments.

I recommend not relying on bank valuations for your accounting entries, as you cannot get all their inputs to perform further analysis or substantiate the fair value upon an auditor's request. In the case of Effectiveness testing, as covered in the next chapter, you will also need to create a hypothetical derivative and generate a fair value for the hypothetical. Therefore, having access to a fair value measurement tool or treasury management system is critical. This will allow you to own all the inputs and outputs and quickly disseminate the make-up of the fair value number to be used in your accounting entries.

Foreign Exchange Forward Contracts

This section will focus on the Foreign Exchange Forward contract, commonly called a Forward Exchange Contract

(FEC) or FX Forward. I will provide their definition and methodology used to measure their fair value and the typical journals you would post into the general ledger.

When applying hedge accounting for foreign exchange risk, the FX Forward is the most popular hedging instrument used in the market by some considerable distance. These instruments are widely understood even by less sophisticated users and qualify for hedge accounting treatment.

An FX forward contract is a financial instrument that enables two parties to agree to exchange a specific amount of one currency for another at a predetermined exchange rate on a future date. The contract specifies the currencies involved, the amount to be exchanged, the agreed-upon exchange rate, and the maturity or settlement date. Unlike spot transactions that occur immediately, forward contracts are settled at a future date, typically ranging from a few days to several years.

The forward contract allows the parties involved to hedge against potential fluctuations in currency exchange rates, providing stability and certainty in future balance sheet valuations and cash flows.

As the definition above states, the future cash flows are known in advance; the contract rate has been locked in. The fair value measurement of an FX Forward is done by comparing the contract rate with the current forward rate in the market.

At each measurement date, the contract will either be In-The-Money (ITM) or Out-The-Money (OTM), depending on the forward rate relative to the fixed contract rate. This will depend on whether the FX rate has moved for or against you, and the fair value should be discounted back into present-day value.

How do we determine whether the hedge is in-the-money?

For example, an Australian exporter selling into the US market has forecasted a surplus of USD to sell. It locks in a contract rate to sell USD buy AUD in three months. In two months, the AUD/USD rate is near parity, resulting in the hedge being In-The-Money as the AUD has strengthened.

Should the exporter decide to close out the position early, it would buy the same amount of USD and sell AUD using the market forward rate. The USD amounts net to zero, and the exporter is left with surplus AUD as the close-out AUD amount is less than the hedged rate, representing the gain on the contract, which is discounted back into present-day value.

Let's add some numbers to this example:

The exporter agrees with the bank to Sell USD 80 at AUD/USD 0.80 and Buy AUD 100 in three months. The AUD/USD exchange rate then moves to parity, i.e. AUD/USD 1.00; they would only receive AUD 80 if unhedged, so you are technically In-The-Money (benefiting) with the hedging derivative in place. If the exporter closed out the position at parity, it would generate a gain on the hedge of AUD 20.

The accounting journals and treatment undertaken for a derivative differ depending on the hedge designation. In Chapter 1, we discussed the different types of hedge relationships.

Fair Value Hedges

The gains or losses on the derivative contract should be recorded on the balance sheet, with the other side of the journal going into the profit or loss account. Suppose the hedged item on the balance sheet must still be measured at fair value. In that case, the carrying amount should be adjusted to offset the movement on the derivative, with the other side of the journal going to profit or loss.

A fair value hedge that qualifies for hedge accounting treatment is accounted for as follows:

Description	Classification	Debit	Credit
Fair value of derivative	Balance Sheet	X	
Unrealised gains or losses	PnL		X
Being the unrealised gain on the derivative			

Description	Classification	Debit	Credit
Unrealised gains or losses	PnL	X	
Cost Basis Adjustment	Balance Sheet		X
Being hedged item carry adjustment			

In this case, the gain on the hedge offsets the movement in the hedged item in profit or loss. The cost basis adjustment will adjust the carrying amount if the hedged item is recognised on the balance sheet. If the hedge is an unrecognised firm commitment, the above movement is still recorded, and the hedged item's fair value is recognised as an asset or liability.

Cash Flow Hedges

The derivatives' unrealised gains or losses can be accumulated in the Cash Flow Hedge Reserve in Other Comprehensive Income (OCI) until the highly probable forecast transaction impacts profit or loss when a reclassification adjustment is undertaken.

The hedged item can either be an unrecognised forecast transaction or relate to a future interest payment on a floating rate loan, and therefore, the gains or losses on the hedging instrument are accumulated in OCI to remove profit or loss volatility, with no offset on the hedged item available until the future interest payments impact profit or loss.

A cash flow hedge that qualifies for hedge accounting treatment is accounted for as follows:

Step 1:

Description	Classification	Debit	Credit
Fair value of derivative	Balance Sheet	X	
Unrealised gains or losses	PnL		X
Being the unrealised gain on the derivative contract			

Step 2:

Description	Classification	Debit	Credit
Unrealised gains or losses	PnL	X	
Cash flow Hedge Reserve/OCI	Balance Sheet		X
Being the accumulation of gains or losses in OCI			

Step 3:

Description	Classification	Debit	Credit
Cash flow Hedge Reserve/OCI	Balance Sheet	X	
Hedged Line-item in PnL	PnL		X
Reclassification adjustment			

Suppose the hedged forecast transaction is a non-financial asset or liability. In that case, the hedge of foreign currency inventory, then amounts deferred in OCI, should be removed and applied directly as a basis adjustment of the inventory when the inventory has been recognised on the balance sheet. The journal for Step 3 would, therefore, change to:

Step 3:

Description	Classification	Debit	Credit
Cash flow Hedge Reserve/OCI	Balance Sheet	X	
Cost Basis Adjustment of Inventory	Balance Sheet		X
Being hedged item carry adjustment			

The gain or loss on the hedge is then released to profit or loss when the corresponding hedged inventory is sold.

Step 4:

Description	Classification	Debit	Credit
Inventory	Balance Sheet	X	
Cost of Goods Sold	PnL		X
Being journal to reflect inventory sold			

There are further accounting mechanics to discuss cash flow hedges around hedge ineffectiveness and the treatment of the amounts deferred in OCI. This is covered in chapters 5 and 8, respectively.

This section focuses on the Foreign Exchange Forward contract (FEC) or FX Forward, providing a comprehensive understanding of its definition, fair value measurement methodology, and accounting treatment. The FX Forward contract is widely used as a hedging instrument to manage foreign exchange risk in businesses exposed to currency fluctuations. The fair value of an FX Forward is determined by comparing the contract rate with the current forward rate in the market, considering whether the contract would be In-The-Money (ITM) or Out-The-Money (OTM) if closed out at the measurement date.

The accounting treatment for FX Forward contracts differs based on the hedge designation. In fair value hedges, the contract's fair value gain or loss is recorded on the balance sheet, with the corresponding journal entry impacting the profit or loss account. For cash flow hedges, the fair value gain or loss can be accumulated in other comprehensive income (OCI) until the forecasted foreign currency sales or purchases affect the profit or loss statement, requiring a reclassification adjustment. In some instances, where the hedge involves non-financial assets or liabilities, such as foreign currency inventory, the amounts deferred in OCI are removed and directly adjusted as a basis for the inventory recognition on the balance sheet.

Interest Rate Swaps

This section covers the accounting journals typically posted for interest swaps and how their fair values are measured. The most common journals to post are valuations, interest accruals, and net settlements. We will also discuss the differences between clean and dirty prices. This section defines an IRS and a table of cash flows used to ascertain the NPV or fair value.

Interest rate swaps (IRS) are very common hedging instruments used to manage fluctuations in interest rates. It's a contract between two parties who agree to exchange interest rate payments over a set period. The two parties typically exchange fixed-rate and floating-rate interest payments based on a notional principal amount in this arrangement. The party paying the fixed interest rate often seeks protection against potential interest rate increases. The fair value of an interest rate swap is determined by considering the present value of expected future cash flows remaining. Therefore, it's the estimated value of the swap if it were to be terminated or sold in the market at current rates. The NPV or MTM is then the sum of all the cash flows on the

Floating Leg minus the Fixed Leg. If you are due to receive the larger one out of the two in the Leg, this will be ITM or an Asset in your books.

I've represented this valuation technique in the table below.

KEVIN MITCHELL

Floating Leg

Floating leg Number	Effective Date	Maturity Date	Notional	Rate	Cashflow	Present Value
1	30 Dec 2022	30 Mar 2023	105,000,000.00	3.30000%	854,383.56	847,137.59
2	30 Mar 2023	30 Jun 2023	105,000,000.00	3.75858%	994,735.99	977,166.47
3	30 Jun 2023	29 Sep 2023	105,000,000.00	4.196684%	1,098,611.04	1,068,162.75
4	29 Sep 2023	29 Dec 2023	105,000,000.00	4.38185%	1,147,084.92	1,103,376.75
5	29 Dec 2023	28 Mar 2024	105,000,000.00	4.34708%	1,125,477.53	1,071,242.27
6	28 Mar 2024	28 Jun 2024	105,000,000.00	4.25405%	1,125,865.63	1,060,375.40
7	28 Jun 2024	30 Sep 2024	105,000,000.00	4.19745%	1,135,035.92	1,057,714.71
8	30 Sep 2024	16 Oct 2024	105,000,000.00	4.19556%	193,110.67	179,629.11

Fixed Leg

Floating leg Number	Effective Date	Maturity Date	Notional	Rate	Cashflow	Present Value
1	30 Dec 2022	30 Mar 2023	105,000,000.00	1.37000%	354,698.63	351,690.45
2	30 Mar 2023	30 Jun 2023	105,000,000.00	1.37000%	362,580.82	356,176.36
3	30 Jun 2023	29 Sep 2023	105,000,000.00	1.37000%	358,839.73	348,899.93
4	29 Sep 2023	29 Dec 2023	105,000,000.00	1.37000%	358,639.73	344,974.22
5	29 Dec 2023	28 Mar 2024	105,000,000.00	1.37000%	354,698.63	337,606.18
6	28 Mar 2024	28 Jun 2024	105,000,000.00	1.37000%	362,580.82	341,489.94
7	28 Jun 2024	30 Sep 2024	105,000,000.00	1.37000%	370,483.01	345,226.24
8	30 Sep 2024	16 Oct 2024	105,000,000.00	1.37000%	63,057.53	58,655.32

All values are expressed in AUD as per the chosen Valuation Currency. The FX rate is the close of business rate as of 30 Dec 2022 (Valuation Date).

Figure 2 Source: Hedgebookpro

What constitutes a clean or dirty price?

Most third-party valuations provided will include the interest accrual amount as well as the fair value of the swap. Understanding whether the fair value includes or excludes the interest accrual is essential. A 'dirty price' will consist of the interest accrual, and a 'clean price' excludes the accrual.

Why is it important?

The dirty price can be used to track and measure hedge effectiveness. This involves calculating the degree of offset of the interest rate swap versus the hypothetical swap. See the next chapter for more details and examples. However, a clean price is needed when running the IFRS 9 'Lower of' effectiveness tests. This is because only gains and losses deemed effective should be held in the cash flow hedge reserve in OCI. More on the 'Lower of' test later in the next chapter.

As summarised below, various accounting journals are required for interest rate swaps in a hedge relationship for hedge accounting purposes.

Recognition & measurement at fair value

At each reporting date, which might be monthly, quarterly, and so on, the balance sheet needs to reflect the current fair value.

The best practice is to record the clean price and the other side going to the CFHR (if a cash flow hedge) or profit or loss in a fair value hedge. It's much cleaner to separate the interest accrual on the balance sheet. I prefer to post these regular journals as reversing journals.

Interest accruals

The interest rate accrual on the balance sheet is the same as any other interest accrual, for example, a loan payable to a third party. I post these as a reversing journal between the accruals accounts on the balance sheet and the interest expense line in profit or loss. The interest accrual on the underlying debt should offset the swap.

Net settlements

Depending on the interest rate accrual periods, typically one or three monthly, a net settlement will be paid or received between the two parties to the contract. This is a physical cash payment, usually done on a swap-by-swap basis. Still, with a portfolio of swaps with one counterparty, the individual swap amounts can be aggregated to ease the administration. The interest calculation is based on a notional principle, although the notional amounts do not require settling. The journal would be between cash at the bank and the interest expense line in profit or loss, and they will offset the interest paid on the debt facility.

Hedge ineffectiveness

Chapter 5 details the calculation of hedge ineffectiveness for interest rate swaps, which creates an amount that is required to be posted to profit or loss. The testing will uncover the amount deemed effective and to be carried in the CFHR in equity. The ineffectiveness is the balancing amount and will depend on what gains or losses have already been posted to the CFHR.

Options

An option is akin to an insurance policy; it should protect you from downside risks and allow you to participate in favourable market moves. The company has the right but not the obligation to use the option; for this right, the standard practice is to pay a premium. This differs from an FX Forward contract when the cash flows are locked in and certain.

Using an option as a hedging product is not for all. Some CFOs will stay clear of options as they know the board has a preconceived opinion of them or the business has previously used options with negative consequences, most likely under the old accounting standards when the accounting treatment was more restrictive. Under IFRS 9, options products such as zero-cost collars, purchased options, participating forwards and swaptions are regularly used by businesses with good outcomes. The fair value measurement and accounting entries associated with option products are less straightforward, so I wanted to include a section in this chapter specifically on options. In this section, I will define the common types of options in the market and the components that make up the fair value. I will also discuss how you can improve hedge ineffectiveness by designating certain aspects of the option's fair value and the accounting entries to be undertaken.

Most options I see across my client base are hedging foreign exchange or interest rate risks. As discussed in Chapter 1, not all options are eligible for hedge accounting treatment, measured at FVTPL (Fair Value Through Profit or Loss). Here, we will focus on the requirements for the options suitable for hedge accounting.

As mentioned in Chapter 3, when discussing possible sources of ineffectiveness, an option's fair value comprises its intrinsic and time value components. The time value is the balancing number in the following equation:

Total Option Value = Intrinsic Value* + Time Value**

*Intrinsic value = option's exercise price less the spot price.

**Time value = Total Option Value less Intrinsic Value.

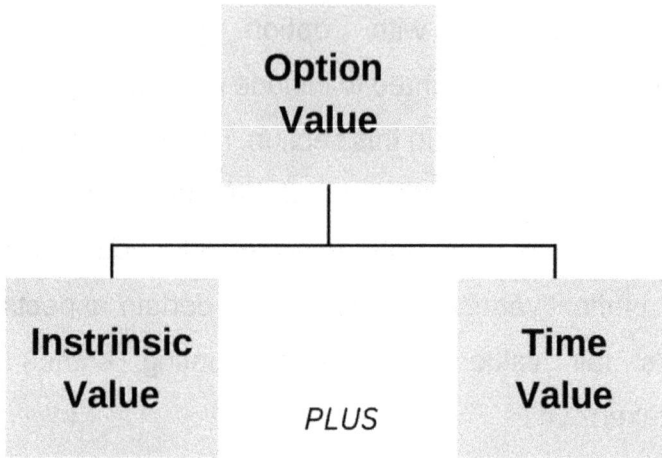

Figure **3**: Option Equation Diagram

Using round numbers, if the client enters a call option to buy gold at US$1,000,000 at a date in the future, but the current cost at the spot price is US$1,500,000, then the option's intrinsic value is US$500,000. If the total fair value of the option is measured at $600,000, then the time value would be the difference of US$100,000. Note at expiry, an option will have no time value.

Intrinsic Value	=	$500,000
Time Value	=	$100,000
Total Fair Value	=	$600,000

Accounting Treatment of Time Value

Under the previous standard, the movements in the fair values relating to time value used to be recorded in profit or loss, creating unwanted volatility. However, IFRS 9 allows the time value to be initially recorded within OCI and subsequent movements contained here. Ultimately, the time value is recognised in profit or loss on a cost basis depending on the nature of the hedged item and the relationship of the time value to the hedged item.

If the hedged item is transaction-related, once the transaction occurs, the gains or losses relating to the intrinsic value are capitalised as a basis adjustment. The option premium is viewed as a cost of hedging and capitalised as well. A transaction-related hedge is hedging a future transaction, i.e. a forecast purchase of inventory.

The accounting entries example below are for a 'transaction-related' hedged item. The importer is hedging the future costs of foreign currency inventory and buys an option for $10,000 to hedge the risk. This option allows the importer to cap the purchase price at $666,667. With the premium included, this brings an all-in cost of $676,667.

It should be noted the importer would have the 'option' to trade at the prevailing market rate at settlement if this is a better outcome and doesn't need to exercise the option.

	Cash	Option	Inventory	CFHR – Intrinsic value	CFHR – Time value	CoGS
Option premium (cash paid)	10,000	10,000				
FV changes		50,000		47,619	2,381	
Purchase of material at spot	714,286		714,286			
FV changes		12,381			12,381	
Settlement of Option at MT	47,619	47,619				
Reclassify the FV to Inventory			47,619	47,619		
Capitalise the initial TV to Inventory			10,000		10,000	
Transfer to CoGS			676,667			676,667
	676,667	-	-	-	-	676,667

Figure 4 Source: CA ANZ Perspective case study

If the hedge is time-period related, i.e. it's not transaction related, an example being a net investment hedge of foreign operations for FX risk or an Interest Rate Cap hedging the interest payable on a floating rate bank facility, the accounting entries are more straightforward. The time value is accounted for as follows:

The initial time value at inception, usually equal to the premium, is amortised to profit or loss over the hedge term on a straight-line or more appropriate basis. Subsequent movements in the time value are contained within OCI in a separate equity component.

Credit Risk Adjustments to Valuations

This subject becomes more relevant the larger your book of derivatives gets. As touched on in Chapter 3, the impact of credit risk on the movements to the overall fair value needs to be assessed when preparing the hedge relationship documentation. This section will investigate what factors increase or decrease credit risk in your positions and the methodology behind constructing the risk curves required to make these adjustments. We will also cover the Credit Valuation Adjustments (CVA), Debit Valuation Adjustments (DVA) and examples of the valuation adjustment journals.

In accordance with IFRS 13 – Fair Value Measurement, there is a requirement to reflect the non-performance risk in the fair value of one party to the financial derivative causing financial loss to the other. Any changes to one of the party's credit ratings should be considered along with any other related circumstances.

What factors would increase the credit risk when considering CVA and DVA adjustments?

I've listed some below:

- Credit rating or credit spread of both parties

- Inability to net off similar exposures

- When no collateral has been posted

- Trades with long maturity dates

- Significant books in terms of MTM and nationals

- Black swan events

Methodologies used:

The Complex Approach (i.e. used by Banks)

CVA is often calculated using the formula:

Exposure x Probability of Default x Loss Given Default

The credit risk formula most banks use is the 'Exposure at Default' (EAD) model. It helps banks estimate the potential loss on a loan or credit exposure based on three key factors:

Exposure (EAD)

Exposure represents the total funds or credit extended to a borrower or counterparty. It is the value of the loan or credit facility at a specific point in time, considering any outstanding principal, accrued interest, and other relevant components. In other words, it is the total financial value at risk in the event of default.

Probability of Default (PD)

The Probability of Default (PD) refers to the likelihood or chance that a borrower or counterparty will fail to meet their debt obligations and default on their credit facilities. It is expressed as a percentage and represents the probability of default within a specific time horizon (e.g., one year). The PD is typically based on historical default rates, credit scores, financial ratios, and other relevant indicators.

Loss Given Default (LGD)

Loss Given Default (LGD) represents the proportion of the exposure expected to be lost if the borrower or counterparty defaults. In other words, it measures the potential loss on the exposure, given that a default has occurred. LGD is usually expressed as a percentage, and its value depends on various factors, such as collateral held, recovery rates, and other risk mitigation measures.

It's important to note that this formula is just one of several methods banks use to assess credit risk. Other factors, such as the borrower's credit rating, industry trends, economic conditions, and the purpose of the credit facility, are also considered in credit risk assessment. The credit risk model helps banks make informed decisions on lending and managing their overall credit portfolio to minimise potential losses.

Most banks will also base the above calculation on the potential future exposure instead of the current exposure method. This tends to require more sophisticated and expensive proprietary software. Most non-banks are more likely to perform a more simplified approach.

The Simplified Approach

This is undertaken by looking at the current exposure to the reporting entity. Although it's easier to perform and less expensive, the results will be less accurate but acceptable from a capability, materiality, and commercial perspective.

In assessing the reporting entity's credit risk without a credit rating, look at the margin they pay on their financing facility above the risk-free rate offered between banks. This margin will be documented within the agreement with the bank. The bank has assessed your credit risk and offered you funds accordingly at this rate. The margin is typically represented in basis points.

In assessing the counterparty's credit risk, the best method is to build a credit curve over the next few years by looking at the Credit Default Spread (CDS) observable in the market. These are reported on Bloomberg and similar market data platforms. Failing that, you can also look at the coupon rates issued on their corporate bond issuances to reverse engineer the perceived credit risk above a government bond of the same tenor. A Government bond is considered a risk-free rate for this exercise. Due to the perceived lower risk profile, the government bonds coupon rate for the same maturity will be lower than the corporates'. A curve can be built by plotting this variance on a graph at six-monthly intervals up to four to five years out. The credit curve for the reporting entity and the counterparty can be used to estimate the risk-free valuation of the derivative book by applying the credit assumption to the curve used for discounting the future cash flows on the swaps to obtain a hypothetical 'risk-free' valuation.

Credit risk example

ABC Ltd has a forward contract with a bank with an NPV of $1,000,000 in favour of the bank, i.e. Out-The-Money (OTM) for ABC Ltd. There is a credit risk to the bank that, at maturity, ABC Ltd falls into administration and cannot pay the close-out position to the bank. The opposite holds; if the forward contract is In-The-Money for ABC Ltd, there is a credit risk the bank might not be able to perform on the contract due to a credit crunch environment, such as the Global Financial Crisis (GFC) or another systemic black swan event.

CVA & DVA example journal entries

IFRS 13 Fair Value Measurement states that the fair value of the derivative book should reflect the credit risk of the counterparty and the reporting entity. What dictates the accounting entries is whether the hedging instrument is In-The-Money or Out-The Money, i.e., is the derivative an asset to the entity or a liability?

Looking at both these permutations from the perspective of the reporting entity, these are summarised in the table below, together with the associated CVA/DVA classification and journal entries.

Contract position	Balance Sheet	CVA/DVA Classification	Accounting Entry
ITM	Asset	Credit Valuation Adjustment (CVA)	Cr Fair Value Derivative Dr Profit or Loss
OTM	Liability	Debit Valuation Adjustment (DVA)	Dr Fair Value Derivative Cr OCI

In both cases, the fair value amount on the Balance Sheet is reduced by the adjustment for credit risk. The journal for the DVA does not go to Profit or Loss, as this could create a situation whereby you are inflating your reported earnings when your credit risk is increasing.

Counterparty risk mitigation

Some organisations will have restrictions inside their treasury risk management policy on whom they can deal with based on credit ratings and other counterparty metrics.

Hedge ineffectiveness due to CVA/DVA entries

Only credit risk on the hedging instrument is measured for hedge accounting purposes. Therefore, this will become a source of ineffectiveness, with no potential for an offset in profit or loss with the hedged item unless the hedged item is measured at fair value under IFRS 13. This is especially true when hedging a forecast transaction, as the forecast does not represent a contractual agreement with another party.

Summary

In this chapter, I emphasised the importance of fair value measurement and the associated journal entries in achieving accurate financial reporting and compliance with hedge accounting standards. We delved into the classification and measurement requirements for financial derivatives, guided by IFRS 13 and IFRS 9, and explored the intricacies of valuing derivatives and employing the income method. This method involves converting future cash flows into their present value, considering factors like discount rates and credit risk adjustments.

It is essential to grasp that the accounting treatment for derivatives can vary significantly based on their hedge designation. The chapter provided comprehensive insights into the accounting journal entries for interest rate swaps, covering recognition, measurement, interest accruals, and net settlements.

The clean and dirty prices are essential to understand when recording the effective component of a cash flow hedge. Options can be used as effective hedging instruments, especially under the latest hedge accounting standard. By understanding these accounting principles, you can effectively utilise options in hedging strategies while maintaining transparency and compliance with accounting standards.

Chapter 4 – Key Takeaways

- Obtaining two slightly different valuations for the identical derivative is common due to different market data cuts or discount rates.
- An interest rate swap 'dirty price' includes accrued interest, whereas the 'clean' price excludes accrued interest.
- Understanding the difference between a contract that is ITM or OTM is crucial when creating the GL entries.
- The total value of an option is a combination of the intrinsic value and the time value. The time value can be excluded from the hedge designation to improve hedge effectiveness.
- To comply with accounting standard IFRS 13, the valuation of a financial derivative should consider the credit risk associated with the non-performance of the contract.

Chapter 5:
Effectiveness Testing Reports

Introduction

Hedge effectiveness testing is an essential aspect of hedge accounting, ensuring that the changes in the hedge's fair value adequately offset the hedged item's fair value. The variables that test hedge effectiveness constantly change, meaning your testing processes should be undertaken regularly. Undertaking the appropriate hedge effectiveness testing can help you position your business for success. Understanding the critical ways to test your hedge relationships at inception and every reporting period is essential. This chapter delves into the different types of tests available, a deep dive into the hypothetical derivative method and ways to identify and quantify the ineffectiveness of your hedge relationship. The major sources of ineffectiveness are also covered.

The Different Types of Tests

Here, we define what hedge effectiveness means for hedge accounting purposes and the different methodologies undertaken to measure hedge ineffectiveness. I highlight the common oversights and discuss the risks and challenges in this area.

The best description of hedge effectiveness is the degree to which the changes in the fair value of the hedge offset the changes in the hedged item's fair value. Ineffectiveness is, therefore, the differences in that offset.

Some of the requirements for an effective hedge are;

- An economic relationship must exist between the hedge and the hedged item

- Credit risk should not dominate the changes in fair value

- Testing should be undertaken at inception and each reporting date at a minimum

- The most common methods to test hedge effectiveness are a qualitative approach and a quantitative approach.

Qualitative test

If all the key terms match between the hedged item and the hedging instrument, then a qualitative approach is sometimes adequate. Should there be some discrepancies, then a quantitative approach is likely needed.

- A qualitative assessment is made at each reporting period's end to confirm an economic relationship exists.

- The hedging instrument's fair value changes, and the hedged item (hypothetical derivative) are based on the same underlying risk, AUD- BBR-BBSW-1M. Therefore, the hedging instruments and the hedged items are expected to move systematically in the opposite direction and offset each other.

Quantitative tests

Regression and ratio analysis are the most common methods when undertaking quantitative testing.

- **Regression analysis**

    This is better suited when there is basis risk, and your hedged item and hedge have different underlying risks. This is quite common when hedging commodity price risk, and there isn't an active market in the commodity grade that the reporting entity is trying to hedge. Instead, the entity must hedge the exposure with a similar but not identical exposure based on another specific risk, creating basic risk.

    The mechanics of regression analysis involve determining a slope coefficient, which is the slope of the straight line of best fit between two variables. The more data points used, the more robust the testing will be. The number of data points should be sufficient for statistical test reliability and consistent from period to period.

- **Ratio analysis**

This quantitative test is also referred to as the Dollar-offset test. The dollar amounts in fair value of the hedged item and hedging instrument are used to calculate the percentage offset. When hedging a highly probable forecast transaction, valuing the change in fair value of the hedged item requires a specialised system and the use of the hypothetical derivative approach—more on this in the next section.

Occasionally, the reporting entity might have to change the testing method due to a change in circumstances. Although this won't cause the hedge relationship to be discontinued, the documentation should be promptly updated.

Hedge effectiveness testing is crucial to meeting the criteria for obtaining hedge accounting treatment; however, stakeholders and managers need to understand this practice more widely. When your hedge effectiveness testing lacks clarity from the beginning, you risk having continuous errors. Hedge effectiveness testing minimises certain risks of hedging. Without the proper controls, your business has heightened risks of monetary losses over the life of the hedging instrument. Please conduct a thorough testing approach to ensure compliance to avoid your hedge accounting program's cancellation, creating immediate gains and losses on the income statement.

DOWNLOADABLE RESOURCE #6

This checklist has been designed to act as a cheat sheet for finance professionals executing new trades, specifically interest rate swaps (IRS). Unless best practice is followed, hedge accounting can become problematic and risks of hedge ineffectiveness increase, creating more volatility in the profit or loss account.

Download here:

https://www.hedgeeffective.com/hedge-accounting/resources

Hypothetical Derivatives

This section will cover the definition of the hypothetical derivative, what this represents, and why you would use one. We will also discuss the infrastructure needed to run a hypothetical book of the derivatives. Also covered here is the need to have good price visibility when executing trades and why it's important to establish the mid-rate or market rate for each hedge at the time of execution.

With hedge effectiveness testing, for intent and purpose, the hypothetical derivative is an ATM (At-The-Money) swap. This means at inception, the NPV or fair value is zero. The hypothetical swap should match the critical terms of the hedged item. In practice, the hypothetical swap is the same product type as the hedging instrument. For example, if you are hedging with an interest rate swap as your hedging instrument, your hypothetical swap will also be an IRS but one that has a zero NPV on Day 1. To reverse engineer and calibrate the hypothetical derivative to achieve a zero NPV at inception or regularly report on the latest fair values requires specialised treasury infrastructure that most finance teams will not have access to. This is one of the reasons I'm sceptical that most entities can measure hedge ineffectiveness in the first place, never mind generating the accounting entries needed. Using a hypothetical derivative approach is very common when hedging forecast transactions in a cash flow hedge relationship scenario.

One method of establishing your hypothetical ATM rate is to deal live in the market and get confirmation of the mid-rate at the execution time. For example, you are about to execute an interest rate swap:

IRS Fixed Rate = Market mid-rate + Bank Spread

Mid-rate = a
Bank costs = B
IRS Fixed Rate = a + B

The Hypo rate will = a = Market mid-rate

Quantifying ineffectiveness

When running a hedge accounting program, you need to be able to run effectiveness testing to establish the degree of offset and level of hedge effectiveness, which should help generate the required accounting entries. This is especially true when you believe there is a good chance hedge ineffectiveness exists. Hedge ineffectiveness exists when the Key Terms Matched Test are not 100% the same between the hedged item and hedging instrument.

In this section, we will cover how to measure hedged ineffectiveness, my preferred approach, a description of the 'Lower of test' with example, and how to estimate ineffectiveness due to a 'timing mismatch'. From experience, the capability to run effectiveness testing is a step too far for most internally run programs due to a lack of knowledge and system infrastructure; therefore, if you get familiar with the approaches in this section, you will be ahead of the pack.

Background

When running a hedge accounting program, measuring the fair value changes of the hedged item and the hedging instrument is necessary. To measure the fair value changes of the hedged item, sometimes it's necessary to use a hypothetical derivative. The portfolio of hypothetical derivatives should be recorded separately from your actual hedge book for testing purposes. The fair values should be measured on a net present value basis. Without access to specialised systems, this will be cumbersome to do on a spreadsheet.

Hedge ineffectiveness – what to measure?

From the inception of the hedge relationship, the reporting entity should be measuring the cumulative changes in fair values of both the hedged item and the hedging instrument. Measuring the fair values and any accrued interest is essential at each reporting date. As discussed in Chapter 4, the accrued interest (if any) is important to establish the clean and dirty price.

Lower of test

When performing effectiveness testing for a cash flow hedge relationship, it's recommended to conduct the 'Lower of' test to help generate the general ledger entries for hedge ineffectiveness. The 'Lower of' test will calculate the dollar amount allowed to be held within the Cash Flow Hedge Reserve (CFHR) account in equity. The rule is only the 'Lower (in absolute terms) of' the following amounts can stay in the CFHR as this is deemed the effective portion:

- The cumulative change in fair value of the hedging instrument from inception versus,

- The cumulative change in fair value of the hedged item since inception

It follows that any fair value changes that are deemed ineffective following the Lower of the test are posted to profit or loss. There are occasions when an entry needs to be made to agree to the balance in the CFHR following the 'Lower of' test; the other side of this entry also goes to profit or loss as ineffectiveness. The following example should help:

Reporting Date	Hypothetical Derivative (ATM Swap)			Interest Rate Swap (The Hedging Instrument)				Lesser of Cuml Chg	Ratio	Efct v	PnL Dr/ (Cr)	OCI / CFHR
	Clean FairVal	Periodic Chg	Cuml Chg	Clean FairVal	Hedged Risk	Periodic Chg	Cuml Chg					
01-Sep-21	-	-	-	-657,878	-657,878	-	-	-	100%	YES	657,878	-
31-Dec-21	5,328,485	5,328,485	5,328,485	4,688,701	4,688,701	5,346,579	5,346,579	5,328,485	100%	YES	639,784	5,328,485
31-Mar-22	13,231,851	7,903,367	13,231,851	12,663,495	12,663,495	7,974,794	13,321,373	13,231,851	99%	YES	568,356	7,903,367
30-Jun-22	18,829,215	5,597,364	18,829,215	18,349,959	18,348,959	5,685,463	19,006,837	18,829,215	99%	YES	480,257	5,597,364
												-18,829,215

Calculating Ineffectiveness Due To Timings Mismatch

In hedge accounting, it's common to hedge a group of similar transactions exposed to the same risk. For example, one might use an FX Forward to hedge forecasted sales in a future month. However, the timing mismatch between revenue receipts and the settlement date of the hedging instrument can lead to hedge ineffectiveness. To measure this ineffectiveness, hypothetical FX Forwards can be utilised to clone expected receipt dates, and the difference in fair values at the reporting date can be measured.

In this section on quantifying the ineffectiveness of a hedge accounting program, I have discussed how to conduct effectiveness testing to determine the level of hedge effectiveness. The section emphasises the importance of measuring hedge ineffectiveness, which occurs when the key terms do not fully align between the hedged item and the hedging instrument. The chapter covers various topics, including measuring hedged ineffectiveness, the 'Lower of test' approach with an example, and estimating ineffectiveness due to timing mismatches. Having familiarity with these approaches will give readers an advantage in understanding hedge accounting, as this area is often considered challenging for CFOs and accountants. The chapter also mentions the use of hypothetical derivatives and the importance of measuring fair value changes accurately.

The 80-125% ratio

The topic of the 80-125% ratio still comes up in hedge accounting conversations, even six years after the effective date of IFRS 9 on January 1, 2018. Although this bright-line rule has been removed under IFRS 9, it's still worth noting as it was a significant issue for reporting entities under the previous accounting standard, IAS 39.

IAS 39 had a strict rule that the degree of offset in fair values between the hedged item and the hedging instrument needed to fall within the 80-125% range to be considered highly effective. Moreover, a retrospective lookback period was used to assess if the offset was consistently within the range. This assessment caused profit or loss volatility when hedging relationships were deemed ineffective.

Fortunately, IFRS 9 eliminated this requirement and the retrospective lookback period. Now, the effectiveness of a hedge must be assessed on an ongoing prospective basis using a more qualitative approach. The assessment should be done at a minimum at every reporting date or when there has been a significant change in the hedge relationship.

What is deemed highly effective?

If you suspect any ineffectiveness in the hedge relationship, measuring the degree of offset using the same ratio analysis prescribed by IAS 39 is essential. If the ratio falls outside the range, it doesn't necessarily disqualify the hedge relationship. Still, it should prompt you to conduct further analysis and explore ways to improve the offset going forward. Although some companies specify a certain level of effectiveness required in their hedge accounting policy, it's not mandatory under the accounting standard.

When calculating the degree of offset, it's recommended to use the total fair values, including accrued interest, instead of clean values. However, for performing the 'Lower of' test for cash flow hedges, you should use the clean, fair values instead of the carrying balance of the derivative on the balance sheet. This is because cash transactions that aren't gains or losses may influence the carrying amount. To determine the effective portion to leave in equity, the reporting entity should only consider gains or losses, as only gains or losses affect the profit or loss, not payments or receipts of interest.

Major Sources of Ineffectiveness

The possible sources of hedge ineffectiveness were discussed briefly in Chapter 3, as these should be noted within the hedge relationship documentation form. However, I couldn't have a Chapter on hedge effectiveness testing without delving deeper into the significant sources of ineffectiveness that I see in practice have the most important profit or loss impact, creating unwanted volatility to earnings.

Timing mismatch of cash flows

A timing mismatch between the hedging instrument and the hedged item can create hedge ineffectiveness. When executing an interest rate swap, aligning the swap interest accrual periods to marry the underlying financing accrual periods to improve hedge effectiveness is recommended.

In the case of FX hedging, should the expected date of the underlying foreign currency receipt or payment change, the maturity of the hedging instrument can easily be extended or pre-delivered by using an FX swap to match the exposure settlement date perfectly.

However, when hedging a group of exposures that all impact profit or loss during the month being hedged with a single hedging instrument to minimise transaction costs, there will be ineffectiveness due to the timing mismatch. Determining the level of ineffectiveness can be tricky and requires using the hypothetical derivative approach to estimate the impact of the timing mismatch.

Credit risk

The impact of credit risk was discussed earlier in this chapter. A statement about whether the reporting entity believes credit risk will be significant and how it will be measured is acceptable. The downloadable resource in Chapter 3 gives an example of appropriate working.

Off-market swaps

Designating interest rate swaps that have a non-zero mark-to-market (MTM) at inception will create some ineffectiveness. The degree of which depends on the structure and how close the swap was traded to the mid-rate at the time of execution. A swap, termed a 'blend and extend', is particularly problematic from a hedge accounting perspective and can create significant hedge ineffectiveness. A blend and extend is when you extend an existing swap into a new swap and embed the current MTM into the structure, creating an off-market fixed rate. Before executing a blend and extend, I would always recommend getting a second opinion on the structure and getting the new swap re-priced by an independent party. From a hedge accounting perspective, closing out the old position and executing a new one is cleaner.

On the other hand, from a liquidity position, I can understand why the entity in the loss position might want to roll the loss into the new structure and not take a cash hit. There are some other reasons why a blend and extend is preferred. Still, they are usually not accounting-related and are more about the commercial outcomes and taking a view of the market's future direction.

Off-Market Swap Case Study

A prospective client was unsure why their auditor was questioning a hedge relationship, and specifically, why no hedge ineffectiveness had ever been posted. It turned out the Day 1 fair value of the derivative at the inception of the hedge was causing issues. The interest rate swap was executed as a blend and extend structure which had resulted in the Fixed Rate being 'off-market'. Following our analysis, in comparing the cumulative fair movements of the swap versus an At-The-Money hypothetical swap a significant amount of ineffectiveness was recorded to profit or loss.

Foreign currency basis spread

When hedging with cross-currency swaps, an entity can exclude foreign currency basis spread from the hedge designation to minimise hedge ineffectiveness. This can be relevant when there is no exchange of foreign currency principle for the hedged item, but there is for the cross-currency swap, as the hedged item will not include currency basis risk.

Forward points in a FX Forward contract

Like currency basis spread, when hedging with a forward contract, you can designate only the changes in the spot rate in the hedge relationship to minimise ineffectiveness. For the undesignated forward points component, there is a choice of when the changes in fair value impact profit or loss depending on the nature of the hedged item.

Time value of Options

It is common to exclude the time value of an option from the hedge relationship to minimise hedge ineffectiveness. Only the intrinsic value of the option is designated. The fair value changes relating to time value are accumulated in equity to limit the degree of ineffectiveness to profit or loss. Throughout the hedge, these amounts can be allocated to profit or loss depending on the nature of the hedged item and the linkage to the time value fair value changes.

Interest Rate Floors

If your hedged item and hedging instrument don't have mirroring floors, this should be noted in the documentation as a source of ineffectiveness.

Off-Market Swap Deep Dive

What is an off-market swap? As the name suggests, it's a swap that, at the time of execution, has a net present value (NPV) not equal to zero. For this example, let's assume the hedging instrument is an interest rate swap in a cash flow hedge relationship. Some situations for an off-market swap are discussed below, but this effectively means that the swap contains a charge or financing component built into the structure and future cash flows that represent ineffectiveness. This is because the hypothetical swap used to measure ineffectiveness is an At-The-Money swap; therefore, the fair values movements will not precisely match the actual swap with the finance cost built in. In practice, the fixed leg of the swap is usually higher than that of the hypothetical swap if we assume the reporting entity is paying fixed interest on the swap and receiving floating. Designating an off-market swap is still allowed under IFRS 9, but the accounting impact should be understood early in the piece.

Examples of off-market swaps:

Credit and execution costs

Often referred to as 'costs of hedging' or the costs of doing business, it is the spread the executing partner will apply to the paying leg of the swap, typically the fixed leg. The best practice is to determine the spread before execution and, like with most transactions, try to get quotes from as many providers as possible. These costs are not generally significant and will not significantly impact hedge ineffectiveness. Items that may influence this are the liquidity in the market, length to maturity, size and currency.

Profit-hungry traders, i.e. significant bank spread

Occasionally, there are examples of when an unreasonable amount of bank spread has been added to the cost of the trade. This can create more hedge ineffectiveness and increase overall interest costs across the life of the structure. For example, if an interest rate swap is executed, the trader could quote a higher fixed rate the entity will pay for each calculation period. With a hedge in the hundreds of millions, a 5bps increase in the fixed rate to be paid will increase the net interest expense.

Most traders I've worked with are professional and ethically sound, but like with any measure of society, there are always a few who are not, and you don't want to be on the end of a bad deal for your company. Always price check and reconcile.

Late designation

This can happen when a company wishes to implement a hedge accounting program for a book of swaps that have existed for some time. Hedge accounting can be applied once hedge documentation is created as long as all other criteria are met. However, the Day 1 position of the swaps might be significant and a source of ineffectiveness.

Blend and extends

As mentioned in previous Chapters, this term is used when the MTM of a current swap is built into a new swap. The new swap will have an extended maturity. These structures are more challenging to price check without sophisticated software and can open the door for traders to increase bank spread if you are not careful. Ignoring the bank spread, the current swap will have an NPV, creating ineffectiveness. These structures are, by far and away, the primary source of large ineffectiveness in the hedge relationship. From an accounting perspective, it's much cleaner to close out the existing swap, create a new swap, and amortise the close-out gain or loss from the cash flow hedge reserve over the term of the underlying exposure.

Summary

In Chapter 5, I emphasised the importance of regularly assessing hedge effectiveness to ensure financial strategies yield the desired results. I provided insights into various testing methods, encompassing qualitative and quantitative approaches. Qualitative tests are effective when all key terms align, while quantitative tests involve techniques like regression analysis and ratio analysis.

The chapter also introduced the concept of hypothetical derivatives for measuring hedge effectiveness in cash flow hedge scenarios. I discussed the challenges in measuring ineffectiveness and offered solutions such as the 'Lower of test' and estimating ineffectiveness due to timing mismatches. The transition from the 80-125% ratio, a component of the previous accounting standard (IAS 39), to its removal in IFRS 9 was explained.

Recognising the primary sources of hedge ineffectiveness, including credit risk, basis risk, differences in matched terms, timing mismatches, and off-market swaps, is crucial. Special attention was given to off-market swaps, which can introduce ineffectiveness when measuring hedge effectiveness. If employed, a clear understanding of their accounting impact before execution is essential.

I recommend implementing best practices in hedge execution techniques to minimise unwanted ineffectiveness in hedge relationships, ultimately enhancing the effectiveness of hedge accounting strategies and reducing earnings volatility.

Chapter 5 – Key Takeaways

- Understanding the potential sources of hedge ineffectiveness is crucial to running and effecting hedge accounting program.
- Failure to conduct a quantitative testing of the hedge relationship when ineffectiveness exists can lead to significant PnL volatility when the oversight has been identified.
- Creating a hypothetical book of derivatives plays a pivotal role in being able to measure hedge ineffectiveness of the hedging instruments.

Chapter 6:
Hedge Disclosures

Introduction

This is an area of most importance for first-time adopters of hedge accounting as they are unlikely to have had to disclose any of this information before, especially if they hadn't done any hedging in prior periods. After the first reporting period is complete, the ongoing reporting requirements in future periods will become more straightforward. This chapter provides helpful guidance with examples and a specific focus on sensitivity analysis.

IFRS 7 Hedge Accounting Disclosures

The objective of this accounting standard is to ensure the reporting entity includes sufficient disclosures within their financial statements so the readers of the financial reports can assess the level of risk the reporting entity is exposed to regarding the financial instruments used, the quantum and significance of the instruments used, and the methods used to mitigate the risks.

Prepared correctly and with adequate detail, the disclosures should provide the reader with a more holistic picture of the financial position than if they had only studied the main reports of the balance sheet, profit or loss account, or cash flow statement. Furthermore, the disclosures allow the reporting entity to add specific details about the reporting that is not always immediately clear from the accounts, items such as hedge accounting elections, and other non-mandatory accounting treatments. The more embedded and significant the use of financial instruments within an entity's business model will largely dictate what degree of disclosures are published in the financial statements.

All entities reporting on IFRS and using financial instruments must disclose all the risks arising from those financial instruments. Even if the consolidated parent entity reports on the financial instrument disclosures, the standard still applies to the subsidiary if they hold the financial instruments in their books.

For derivatives that are not designated in a hedge relationship and are therefore carried at fair value through profit or loss, IFRS 7 requires all the changes in fair value and other related income and expenses to be presented in one single line item in profit or loss. The chosen position of the line item of the profit or loss account should stay consistent each reporting period.

Hedge accounting disclosures

Hedge accounting disclosures in a company's financial statements are essential and can be viewed as a link between risk management and financial accounting information.

This table documents the main reason for providing disclosures, including:

Objective	Description
Transparency	Hedge accounting disclosures provide transparency to stakeholders by offering insight into the company's risk management activities. They demonstrate the extent to which the company manages its exposure to various risks, such as foreign exchange rate fluctuations, interest rate changes, or commodity price volatility, and how each of these risks arise in the business. This information allows investors, creditors, and other stakeholders to evaluate the effectiveness of the company's risk management strategies.
Decision-making	The disclosures enable users of the financial statements to make informed decisions. By understanding the company's hedging activities, stakeholders can assess the potential impact of these activities on the company's financial performance and cash flows. This information is crucial for investors and creditors when analysing the company's risk profile and making investment or lending decisions.

Compliance with accounting standards	Hedge accounting disclosures are often required by accounting standards. These standards provide guidelines on how companies should account for and disclose their hedging activities. By including the required disclosures, companies ensure compliance with accounting regulations, promoting consistency and comparability among financial statements.
Risk evaluation	Hedge accounting disclosures allow stakeholders to evaluate the company's risk exposure and the effectiveness of its hedging strategies. They provide information on the types of risks being hedged, the hedging instruments used, the duration of the hedges, and the overall impact on the company's financial statements. This enables stakeholders to assess the company's risk management practices, determine the potential risks that the company is exposed to, and evaluate the success of its hedging activities.

Regulatory requirements	In certain industries, such as banking or insurance, regulatory authorities may require companies to disclose their hedging activities to assess the company's risk profile and compliance with regulatory requirements. These disclosures help regulators monitor and evaluate the company's risk management practices and ensure the stability and soundness of the financial system.

Overall, hedge accounting disclosures provide essential information for stakeholders to understand a company's risk management strategies, make informed decisions, and evaluate its financial performance and risk exposure.

Examples of the qualitative information required

The reporting entity needs to include a description of the following hedge accounting information in the notes to the accounts; most of this information can be taken from the Hedge Relationship Documentation Forms:

- The type of hedging instrument used.

- A description of the economic relationship and how this exists.

- How will the reporting entity measure ineffectiveness and sources of hedge ineffectiveness?

- The amount of notional designated in the hedge relationship.

- Whether the total fair value is hedged or specific components are designated only.

Examples of the quantitative information required

In addition to the qualitative information required on the risk management strategy, the reporting entity must supplement this with some quantitative data. For example, if using FX Forward contracts to uncommitted exposures over the next 24 months, an exporter should provide a table in the accounts breaking down the average rate hedged and the notional sums over specified time buckets.

The following information is usually in the Financial Risk Management Note to the Accounts. The information on the hedging instruments is reported by risk category and type of hedge relationship.

The table below is an extract from IFRS 7 for designated hedging instruments:

	Nominal amount of the hedging instrument	Carrying amount of the hedging instrument		Line Item in the statement of financial position in which the hedged item is included	Change in value used for calculating hedge ineffectiveness for 20X1
		Assets	Liabilities		
Commodity price risk - Forward sales contracts	xx	xx	xx	Line item XX	xx
Interest rate risk - Interest rate swaps	xx	xx	xx	Line item XX	xx
Foreign exchange risk -Foreign currency loan	xx	xx	xx	Line item XX	xx

Figure 6A Source: IFRS 7: IG13C

The following table is an extract from IFRS 7 and relates to the information required for the underlying hedged items:

	Carrying amount of the Hedged Item		Accumulated amount of fair value hedge adjustments on the hedged item included in the carrying amount of the hedged item		Line Item in the statement of financial position in which the hedged item is included	Change in value used for calculating hedge ineffectiveness for 20XX	Cash flow hedge reserve
	Assets	Liabilities	Assets	Liabilities			
Cash flow hedges							
Commodity price risk	n/a	n/a	n/a	n/a	n/a	xx	xx
- Forecast sales	n/a	n/a	n/a	n/a	n/a	n/a	xx
- Discontinued hedges (forecast sales)							
Fair value hedges							
Interest rate risk	--	xx	--	xx	Line item XX	xx	n/a
- Loan payable	--	xx	--	xx	Line item XX	n/a	n/a
- Discontinued hedges (loan payable)							
Foreign exchange risk	xx	xx	xx	xx	Line item XX	xx	n/a
-Firm commitment							

Figure 6B Source: IFRS 7: IG13D

Reconciliation of Other Comprehensive Income (OCI)

IFRS 7 requires the OCI to be reconciled by each risk category that relates to hedge accounting in the same manner and level of detail as provided for the impact of hedge accounting on the profit or loss account. The supporting detail can be shown on the face of the statement of changes in equity or supplementary in the notes to the account.

Statement of changes in equity

Due to the nature of the accounting entries for cash flow and net investment hedges, various equity components are often used to measure gains or losses for hedging instruments in those hedge relationships. This will generate more financial reporting disclosure requirements as changes to each element need to be reconciled in the statement of changes in equity. Separate equity components are common when only specified risk components have been designated in the hedge relationship and when risk components have been excluded, i.e. currency basis spread, time value, and forward points.

Hedge accounting disclosures provide transparency and insight into a company's risk management practices. These disclosures offer several benefits, including transparency to stakeholders, aiding decision-making, compliance with accounting standards, risk evaluation, meeting regulatory requirements, and overall understanding of a company's risk profile.

Qualitative information required in hedge accounting disclosures includes details such as the type of hedging instrument used, description of the economic relationship, measurement of ineffectiveness, and the amount of notional designated in the hedge relationship. This information helps readers understand the nature and purpose of the hedging activities.

Quantitative information complements the qualitative disclosures and may include specific data on hedging instruments, such as average rates hedged and notional amounts over specified periods. This quantitative information provides a more detailed view of the company's hedging strategies and exposures.

Overall, hedge accounting disclosures bridge risk management and financial accounting, offering stakeholders the necessary information to evaluate a company's risk exposure, risk management strategies, and their impact on financial performance.

Sensitivity Analysis

When preparing a set of financial statements, disclosure requirements for sensitivity analysis of foreign exchange rates or interest rates depend on the nature of the reporting entity's operations and jurisdiction. This section provides a general overview of the typical disclosure requirements related to sensitivity analysis of market risks.

A reporting entity should provide a sensitivity analysis that presents the potential impact of changes in foreign exchange rates or interest rates on the entity's financial position, profit or loss, and cash flows. This analysis typically involves using hypothetical scenarios to assess the sensitivity of key financial variables to market risk fluctuations.

The key assumptions used in the sensitivity analysis should be disclosed to assist the readers of the financial statements, such as the percentage changes in exchange rates applied or the period considered. This allows users of the financial statements to understand the basis for the analysis and evaluate its reasonableness.

As all entities applying hedge accounting will be using financial instruments impacted by movements in market rates, disclosures should be provided detailing their sensitivity to foreign exchange rates, interest rates or commodity price fluctuations. This may include information on the instruments' carrying amounts and fair values and the potential impact of fluctuations on their valuation and cash flows.

The percentage changes in the hypothetical scenarios should be reasonable, realistic and ideally consistent from one period to the next.

Personal Anecdote

In my early consulting days, my first-ever hedge accounting customer was busy finalising their annual report and notes to the accounts. In the prior period they had adopted hedge accounting for the very first time and we spent some time creating the disclosures including the sensitivity for movements in FX rates. We estimated the change in fair values should rates move up or down by 5 percent and likely impact on the business in dollar terms. This year-end there was a new accountant in the team who had arrived from another company that was used to sensitivities based on only a 2% change in FX rates and updated the note accordingly. During a review by the auditor, they suggested moving to 5% for consistency and comparability.

This section discusses sensitivity analysis and its disclosure requirements in financial statements. Sensitivity analysis involves assessing the potential impact of foreign exchange or interest rate changes on a reporting entity's financial position, profit or loss, and cash flows. The analysis uses hypothetical scenarios to evaluate the sensitivity of key financial variables to market risk fluctuations. Entities applying hedge accounting, which involves using financial instruments impacted by market rate movements, should provide additional disclosures. The percentage changes in hypothetical scenarios must be reasonable, realistic, and consistent over time. This consistency allows for meaningful comparisons between periods and enhances the reliability of the sensitivity analysis. Remember, these are general guidelines, and the specific disclosure requirements can vary depending on the nature of the entity's operations and the location of headquarters.

Summary

In Chapter 6, I explored the world of hedge accounting disclosures and sensitivity analysis within financial statements. These disclosures are like windows into a company's inner workings, showcasing its risk management activities and strategies, and they offer invaluable transparency to stakeholders. Throughout the chapter, I emphasised the critical role of these disclosures in helping users of financial statements make informed decisions while adhering to accounting standards.

Hedge accounting disclosures serve many purposes, allowing stakeholders to assess a company's risk exposure, evaluate the effectiveness of hedging strategies, and ensure regulatory compliance. I provided examples to illustrate the types of information required, both qualitative and quantitative. Qualitative information includes details about the kind of hedging instruments used, economic relationships, measurement of ineffectiveness, and the amount of notional designated in the hedge relationship. On the quantitative side, I delved into specific data on hedging instruments, such as average rates hedged and notional amounts over specified periods.

Sensitivity analysis is a crucial component of financial analysis. It involves assessing how foreign exchange or interest rate changes impact a company's financial position, profit or loss, and cash flows. It's a vital tool for understanding how external factors can affect a company's financial well-being.

To sum it up, hedge accounting disclosures and sensitivity analysis are essential elements that provide transparency, aid in decision-making processes, and assist in evaluating a company's risk exposure and management strategies. These tools are indispensable for the company and its stakeholders in the complex world of finance.

Chapter 6 – Key Takeaways

- First-year adopters to hedge accounting will find the disclosure requirements more time consuming than regular reporters.
- Disclosing key information in relation to the organizations hedging arrangements is important for the users of financial statements to access the effectiveness of the hedging activities.
- Notes to the accounts are required in a specified format to stay complaint with accounting standards.

Part Three

The final two stages in the eight-step HEDGEHOG method are the Optics of the Financial Reports and GAAP & IFRS Compliance. These two are the outcomes of what a CFO wants when implementing an effective hedge accounting program.

You implement a hedge accounting program to get some form of preferential accounting treatment that will improve the optics of the reported numbers, and you need the accounting to be in accordance with GAAP and IFRS. As the CFO, you always strive to enhance the reporting optics, and staying compliant with the standards is a must.

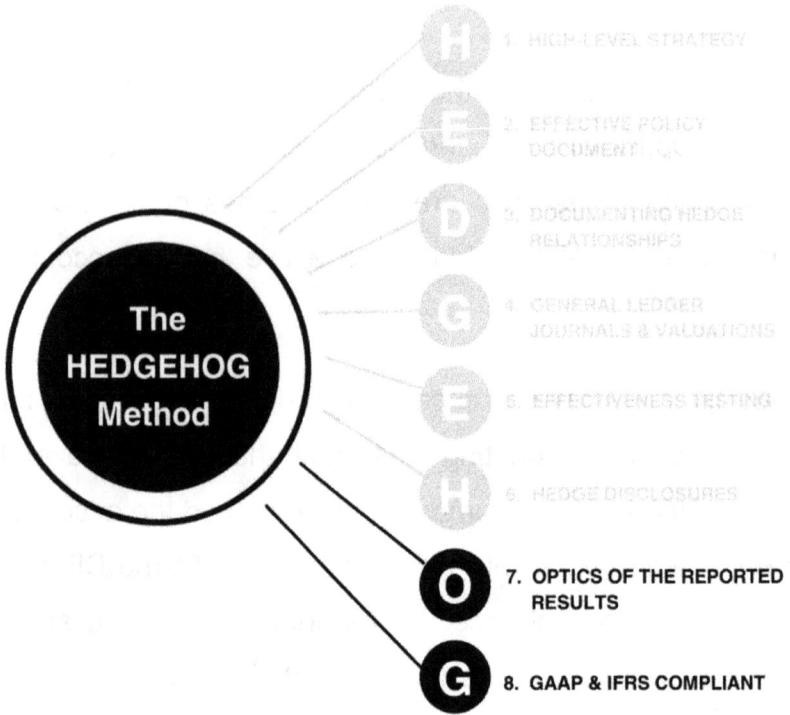

1. HIGH-LEVEL STRATEGY

2. EFFECTIVE POLICY DOCUMENTATION

3. DOCUMENTING HEDGE RELATIONSHIPS

4. GENERAL LEDGER JOURNALS & VALUATIONS

5. EFFECTIVENESS TESTING

6. HEDGE DISCLOSURES

7. OPTICS OF THE REPORTED RESULTS

8. GAAP & IFRS COMPLIANT

Chapter 7:
Optics of the Reported Results

Introduction

This chapter explores the substantial enhancements effective hedge accounting can bring to your reported financial figures. We'll delve into essential topics such as managing financial covenants and understanding the Tax-Of-Financial-Arrangements (TOFA) hedging election. Additionally, I'll share how to accurately reflect the genuine impact of your risk management strategies in your financial statements.

Preferential Accounting Treatment

To mitigate their exposures to market risks, a business will undertake a hedge with a financial derivative to create an offset, thus protecting them from adverse movements. In this section, we will discuss why this can create unwanted financial reporting outcomes and how, by applying hedge accounting, the business can improve the optics in the financial statements. In the previous chapters, we covered more hedge accounting mechanics and compliance requirements. In contrast, this chapter goes straight to the outcome of hedge accounting from a financial reporting perspective.

Even though a financial instrument is taken out to reduce risk, from an accounting perspective, it can create more volatility in earnings. This is generally because the default accounting for a financial derivative is FVTPL, but the underlying exposure may still need to be recorded in the general ledger. This result is far from ideal and causes the financial statements to look distorted, creating difficulties for readers and analysts to get a clear picture of the organisations' earnings and risk profile.

There are some examples below of how hedge accounting attempts to align this mismatch for each reporting period so that the actual underlying performance of the business is not distorted by the hedging undertaken.

The Cash Flow Hedge Reserve (CFHR)

Accounting for cash flow hedges is a considerable benefit for qualifying cash flow hedges. It allows the gains or losses on the hedging instrument, deemed effective, to be deferred in the CFHR until the underlying exposures impact profit or loss. This is a significant benefit to businesses that are hedging two or three years in advance and have no hedged item recorded in their general ledger. Business owners and members of management want to be sure they are making the most informed decisions, which relies on minimising the fluctuations in the PnL. Furthermore, without the application of hedge accounting, market movements must be reported on the PnL. However, with hedge accounting, unrealised gains or losses in designated derivative contracts can be posted to a cash flow hedge reserve, significantly altering your financial statements and reducing PnL volatility.

Presented here is a case study by CS Lucas, a treasury management system with a distinguished track record spanning more than 25 years. First published in 2016, this study stands out as one of the most insightful analyses of the advantages of cash flow hedge accounting, especially for forecasted Accounts Receivables. The case study is fully reproduced below with permission.

Case Study: Trade Receivables

This case study considers the impact of exchange rate movement on foreign currency receivables. It explains the undesirable effects on accounting when a Forward Foreign Exchange (Forward FX) contract is used to hedge exchange rate risks. It outlines the optional provision under IFRS 9 that allows an entity to mitigate these consequences through Hedge Accounting.

For illustration purposes, this guide refers to the following case study as 'the Case'.

Case study details:

- The legal entity is a registered Singapore company.

- The reporting currency of the entity is SGD.

- The entity has entered a 5-year supply contract with a customer in the UK.

- The entity expects to receive GBP 12,500,000 annually.

The following collection is from 15-Mar-2017.

Whilst this guide considers cash receivables, the concepts may equally apply to payables and hedging with a Non-Deliverable Forward contract.

Understanding the impact of volatile exchange rates

Exchange rates fluctuate from day to day and may trend up or down. Below is the pattern of the GBP/SGD rate in 2016.

GBP/SGD Rates 2016

The impact of such fluctuations brings uncertainty to cash flow and profitability. This is illustrated as follows:

- Using the Case and the current date, 13-Jul-2016, the GBP/SGD exchange rate is 1.7938.

Based on this rate, the company would receive SGD 22,422,500. But if there is an adverse movement in the exchange rate of 1%, the loss would be as follows:

GBP Rate	Example	SGD	Impact (SGD)
Depreciates 1%	1.77586	22,198,275	(224,225)

As it turns out, the rate on 15-Mar-2017 was 1.7273. The impact would have been an adverse cash variance of SGD 830,000!

Hedging exchange rate risks with Forward FX contracts

To minimise the impact of volatile exchange rates on receivables, a company can enter into a contract to buy and sell a particular currency at an agreed rate on a future date. That rate would not be the same as the current rate (like 1.7939 in the example above), but it would be fixed at the outset of the contract. With a Forward FX contract, the entity can fully 'immunise' its cash flow from changes in exchange rates going forward. This is illustrated as follows:

The entity enters into a Forward FX contract to sell GBP 12,500,000 in exchange for SGD to be settled on 15-Mar-2017. A bank quotes a rate of 1.8123, to which the entity agrees.

On 15-Mar-17, the entity received GBP 12,500,000 from the UK customer. This is then sent to the financial institution to be converted under the Forward FX contract at the agreed rate of 1.8123. In turn, the entity received SGD 22,653,750.

Proceeds from	GBP	SGD
Sales Contracts	12,500,000	
Forward FX Contract @1.8123	(12,500,000)	22,653,750
Net cash flow	-	22,653,750

Notice that this receipt of SGD is independent of the exchange rate on the day it received the GBP from the UK customer. The amount of SGD it receives is now secure.

What if the market rate on 15-Mar-2017 was 1.9000, higher than 1.8123? The company would still receive SGD 22,653,750 under the Forward FX contract; there is certainty about the SGD amount. The company has missed the opportunity to sell the GBP in the market to receive a more considerable amount of SGD. But, it is not the entity's objective to speculate but to secure a fixed SGD amount under the contract.

Accounting for Forward FX contracts

The Forward FX contract is considered a financial derivative. Under IAS 39 and IFRS 9, a derivative must be initially measured at fair value and subsequent value changes are recognised in profit or loss.

In the context of a Forward FX contract, this means that any unrealised gains and losses must be recognised in the Profit and Loss (PnL) Account at each reporting date.

Computation of unrealised gains/losses

To compute a Forward FX contract's unrealised gain/loss, we compare the contracted exchange rate (1.8123) with the prevailing forward rate for the remaining tenor.

From this guide, we shall assume that the prevailing forward rate on 31-Jul-2016 is 1.8204.

The unrealised gain/loss is the difference between a) the proceeds in SGD selling the GBP 12,500,000 under the contract and b) the proceeds at the prevailing market rate.

This is illustrated as follows:

	Market Rate	Proceeds (b) Market Rate	Proceeds (a) Contracted	Gains/ (Losses)
31-Jul-16	1.8204	22,755,192	22,653,750	(101,442)

The loss of SGD 101,422 implies that the rate we contracted with the bank is not favourable compared with the prevailing market rate. In other words, the obligations under our Forward FX contract are unfavourable to the extent that SGD 101,422 would be a fair value to compensate another to take over such obligations.

Accounting for the monthly unrealised gains/losses

The loss above needs to be reflected in the financial statements.

Below is a summary of the month-end revaluation journal for the loss:

Post Date	Account		Ccy	Dr/(Cr)	Base	Dr/(Cr)
31-Jul-17	FRX: Derivative Liability Fair Value	B/S	SGD	(101,422)	SGD	(101,422)
31-Jul-17	FX: Unrealized Losses — FX Trade	P/L	SGD	101,422	SGD	101,422

The highlighted second entry recognises the loss in the PnL as required under IFRS.

The above is the unrealised loss for the first month of the Forward FX contract, which started on 15-Jul- 2016. For each month, the unrealised gains and losses must be recalculated, and changes (positive and negative) during the month need to be recognised in the PnL until the end of the Forward FX contract.

Below is the gross unrealised to date and the monthly movement using representative revaluation rates at each month's end.

Month End	Period	Cumulative	Rate Used
31-Jul-16	(101,250)	(101,250)	1.8204
31-Aug-16	(22,500)	(123,750)	1.8222
30-Sep-16	252,500	128,750	1.8020
31-Oct-16	990,000	1,118,750	1.7228
30-Nov-16	(957,500)	161,250	1.7994
31-Dec-16	76,250	237,500	1.7933
31-Jan-17	82,500	320,000	1.7867
28-Feb-17	433,750	753,750	1.7520

Graphical representation of the period movement is as follows:

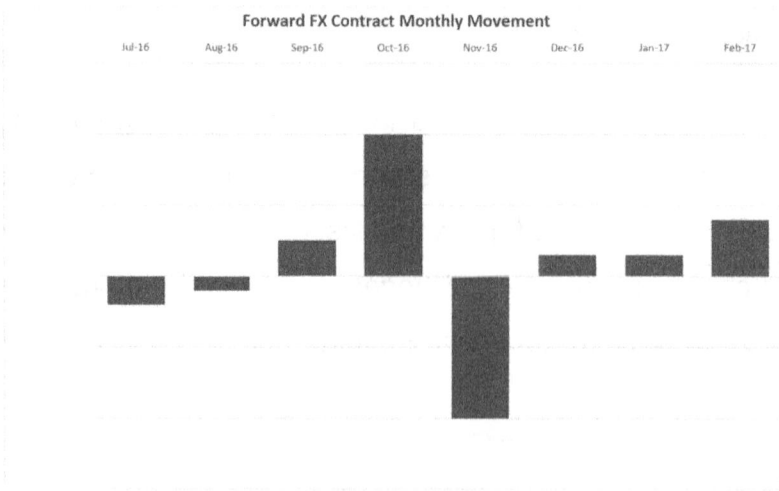

Forward FX Contract Monthly Movement

The above indicates reported profit and loss fluctuation when applying IFRS accounting treatment to Forward FX contracts and exchange rate movement.

Accounting for Account Receivables (A/R)

When a forecast crystalises and becomes an A/R, it would be recorded in the equivalent based currency amount using the prevailing 'book' rate. At each period's end, the accounting system will automatically revalue any unpaid GBP receivables using the period's current rate and restate the base carry amount. This is called monetary asset adjustment, a standard practice for all monetary items, including A/R, A/P, loans and deposits.

Monetary asset adjustments significantly offset the gains and losses arising on the Forward FX contract revaluation above. This is illustrated in the following table

| Month End | Forward FX Contract | | A/R Revaluation | | Monetary | P/L | |
	Period	Fwd Rate	@ HRate	@ M/End Rate	Asset Adj'm	Net Impact	Volatility
31-Jul-16	-101,250	1.8204				-101,250	High
31-Aug-16	-22,500	1.8222				-22,500	(Pre-invoice)
30-Sep-16	252,500	1.802				252,500	
31-Oct-16	990,000	1.7228				990,000	
30-Nov-16	-957,500	1.7994				-957,500	
31-Dec-16	76,250	1.7933	22,231,250	22,210,000	-21,250	55,000	Low
31-Jan-17	82,500	1.7867	22,231,250	22,190,000	-41,250	41,250	(Post-Invoice)
28-Feb-17	433,750	1.752	22,231,250	21,818,750	-412,500	21,250	

Note the month of Feb 2017, when the gross revaluation gains on the Forward FX contract is SGD 433,750, offset by the revaluation losses of A/R to the tune of SGD (412,500). The net impact is only SGD 21,250. The offset could be better because the Forward FX contract was revalued using the forward rate, whereas the A/R was at the spot reference rate. The difference is due to forward points premium or discount on a Forward FX contract. This tends to zero as the trade nears settlement.

The conclusions are:

- Where foreign currency amounts are concerned, the economic impact of exchange rate risk is the same whether it is a forecast or an A/R.

- Whether a forecast or an A/R, a Forward FX contract would be an economically effective hedge for an entity to consider as a risk management strategy.

- Unlike A/R, however, a forecast will not give rise to mirroring journals to offset those from the Forward FX contract. This asymmetric accounting treatment causes fluctuation in reported earnings.

- An entity would only need to elect for Hedge Accounting in the case of a hedge against a forecast but not on A/R or A/P.

Hedge accounting principles

In the previous sections, it is shown that whilst a Forward FX contract is an effective hedge against exchange rate volatility that impacts cash flow, it gives rise to undesirable fluctuation in reported Profit and Loss Accounts under IFRS treatment of financial instruments that we have considered up to this point.

The standard-setting authority recognises this situation, and a provision is made in IFRS 9 (and earlier in a slightly different form in IAS 39) to allow the entity to mitigate the effect by adopting Hedge Accounting.

The company may defer the unrealised gain/loss of Forward FX contracts to the Hedge Reserve account on the balance sheet instead of impacting reported profit and loss.

The Hedge Reserve balance is then released systematically to the PnL Account so sales (A/R) are correctly stated at the hedged rate instead of the usual booked rate.

Hedge Accounting Treatment

Under IFRS 9, the gains and losses on a Forward FX contract in a cash flow hedge may be reclassed from the PnL Account to a Hedge Reserve account on the Balance Sheet. Therefore:

Post Date	Account		Ccy	Dr/(Cr)	Base	Dr/(Cr)
31-Jul-17	FRX: Derivative Liability Fair Value	B/S	SGD	(101,250)	SGD	(101,250)
31-Jul-17	FX: Unrealized Losses — FX Trade	P/L	SGD	101,250	SGD	101,250
31-Jul-17	FX: Unrealized Losses — FX Trade	P/L	SGD	(101,250)	SGD	(101,250)
31-Jul-17	FRS9: Hedge Reserve	BS	SGD	101,250	SGD	101,250

The shaded rows show the reclass from the FX: Unrealised Losses — FX Trade Account to the Hedge Reserve Account (a balance sheet item). The net impact to the P & L is nil.

When the hedged item becomes a sales or cost of a sales item, the deferral to the balance sheet is systematically released to the P & L Account.

Over the life cycle of hedging, the cumulative gains and losses that impact the P & L Account are the same whether or not the entity exercises the option for Hedge Accounting. However, the profile of the impact is dramatically different. Graphically, this is represented as follows:

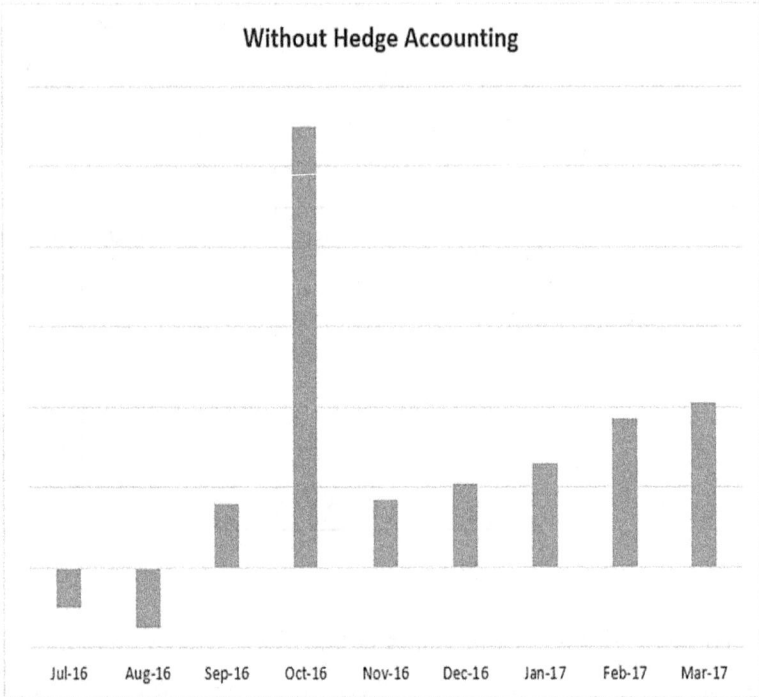

Without Hedge Accounting

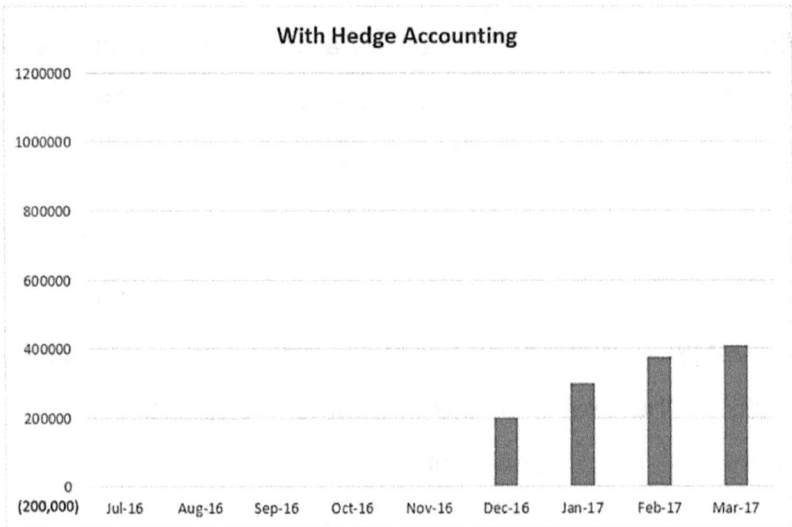

With Hedge Accounting

Hedge Accounting Life Cycle

We will consider Hedge Accounting using the Case. We will illustrate the accounting over the hedging life cycle covering a period from July 2016 to March 2017:

Forecast/Inception	Jul-16 to Dec-16, 2016
Invoicing	Dec-16, 2016
Settlement	Mar 17, 2017

This guide outlines the journals and substantiates essential account balances in each phase. Additional information to the Case and necessary for the illustration of the journals are as follows:

FX Forward Trade Details:

Trade Date	13-Jul-16
Value Date	15-Mar-17
Bought	SGD 22,653,750
Sold	GBP 12,500,000
Contract Rate	1.8123

Exchange Rates and Forward FX Contract Revaluation

Dates	Closing Rate	Bank FX Revaluation
31-Jul-16	1.7794	(101,250.00)
31-Aug-16	1.7862	(123,750.00)
30-Sep-16	1.7710	128,750.00
31-Oct-16	1.6968	1,118,750.00
30-Nov-16	1.7784	161,250.00
31-Dec-16	1.7768	237,500.00
31-Jan-17	1.7752	320,000.00
28-Feb-17	1.7455	753,750.00
23-Mar-17	1.7473	

Forecast/Forward FX Inception

On Jul 16, the company established a highly probable forecast of GBP 12,500,000 and took out the Forward FX contract to sell this at 1.8123 in return for SGD 22,653,750 for the value date 15-Mar-17. The company elected for Hedge Accounting.

On 31-Jul-2016:

		Balance Sheet		Profit & Loss
Post Date	Description	Derivative Asset/(Liab.)	Hedge Reserve	Unrealized FX (Gain)/loss
31-Jul-16	FX Forward Reval	(101,250)		101,250
31-Jul-16	Hedging Reclass		101,250	(101,250)
		(101,250)	101,250	-
	Representing	Fair value of derivative	Deferred loss on derivative	No impact P/L

On 31-Aug-216:

| Post Date | Description | Balance Sheet | | Profit & Loss |
		Derivative Asset/(Liab.)	Hedge Reserve	Unrealized FX (Gain)/loss
1-Aug-16	[Rev] FX Forward Reval	(101,250)		(101,250)
1-Aug-16	[Rev] Hedging Reclass		(101,250)	101,250
31-Aug-16	FX Forward Reval	(123,750)		123,750
31-Aug-16	Hedging Reclass		123,750	(123,750)
	Activity in Aug	(22,500)	22,500	
	Activity to date	(123,750)	123,750	
	Representing	Fair value of derivative	Deferred loss on derivative	No impact P/L

Reversing journals are used; period activities are computed by changes in cumulative balances between period ends.

1-Sep-2016 to 30-Nov-2016:

Unrealised gains/losses on the revaluation of the Forward FX contract continue to be reclassed at month-end, so there is no impact on the P & L Account.

Invoices

In this phase, during the hedging life cycle, an invoice is issued to the UK supplier. This happened during the month of December, using a booked rate of 1.7785.

Dec-2016:

Post Date	Description	Balance Sheet			Profit & Loss		
		Derivative Asset/(Liab)	Hedge Reserve	A/R	Sales	Unrealized FX	Cost of Sales
01-Dec-16	B/F from Nov	161,250	-161,250				
01-Dec-16	[Rev] FX Forward Reval	-161,250					
01-Dec-16	[Rev] Hedging Reclass		161,250				
15-Dec-16	Invoice at spot rate [1]			22,231,250	-22,231,250		
31-Dec-16	Invoices reval'n			-21,250		21,250	
31-Dec-16	FX Forward Reval	237,500				-237,500	
31-Dec-16	Carry Value Adjustment					422,500	-422,500
	Activity in Dec	76,250	161,250	22,210,000	-22,231,250	206,250	-422,500
	Activity to date	237,500	237,500	22,210,000	-22,231,250	206,250	-422,500
	Representing	Fair value of derivative	All Release to P/L	A/R balance at current rate	Sales recognized	See Note [1]	See Note [2]

Note 1:

The invoice revaluation loss is computed as follows:

GBP	SGD @ Current	SGD @ Booked	Gain/(Loss)
	1.7768	1.7785	
12,500,000	(22,210,000)	(22,231,250)	(21,250)

The overall FX loss represents the swap points implied in the Forward FX contract.

	GBP	SGD @ Contract	Bank Fwd ME Spot	Gain/(Loss)
Revaluation Bank	(12,500,000)	1.8123	1.7933	237,500
Revalue to Spot	(12,500,000)	1.8123	1.7768	443,750
			165 points	(206,250)

Note 2:

The reclass of unrealised gains:

GBP	SGD @ Contract	SGD @ Booked	Gain/(Loss)
	1.8123	1.7785	
12,500,000	(22,653,750)	(22,231,250)	422,500

Jan-2017

Post Date	Description	Balance Sheet		A/R	Profit & Loss		
		Derivative Asset/(Liab)	Hedge Reserve		Sales	Unrealized FX	Cost of Sales
01-Jan-17	B/F from Dec	237,500		22,210,000	-22,231,250	206,250	-422,500
01-Jan-17	(Rev) Invoices reval'n			21,250		-21,250	
01-Jan-17	(Rev) FX Forward Reval	-237,500				237,500	
31-Jan-17	Invoices reval'n			-41,250		41,250	
31-Jan-17	FX Forward Reval	320,000				-320,000	
	Activity in Dec	82,500		-20,000		-62,500	
	Activity to date	320,000		22,190,000	-22,231,250	143,750	-422,500
	Representing	Fair value of derivative	All Release to P/L	A/R balance at current rate	Sales recognized	See Note [1]	

Note 1:

The invoice revaluation loss is computed as follows:

GBP	SGD @ Current	SGD @ Booked	Gain/(Loss)
	1.7752	1.7785	
12,500,000	22,190,000	22,231,250	(41,250)

The overall FX loss represents the swap points implied in the Forward FX contract.

	GBP	SGD @ Current	SGD @ Booked	Gain/(Loss)
Revaluation Bank	(12,500,000)	1.8123	1.7867	320,000
Revalue to Spot	(12,500,000)	1.8123	1.7752	463,750
			356 points	(143,750)

Settlement
Mar-2017:

The invoice realised loss is computed as follows:

GBP	SGD @ Current	SGD @ Booked	Gain/(Loss)
	1.7473	1.7785	
12,500,000	21,841,250	22,231,250	(390,000)

The cash settlement of the Forward FX Contract and the resulting gain are as follows:

Ccy	Ccy Amount	Book Rate	Base Amount
SGD	22,653,750.00	1.0000	22,653,750.00
GBP	(12,500,000.00)	1.7473	(21,841,250.00)
		Gain/(Loss)	812,500.00

Source: CS Lucas - https://www.cslucas.com

This excellent case study by CS Lucas demonstrates the benefits of utilising the cash flow hedge reserve to quarantine the unrealised gains or losses on the FX Forward contracts when hedging future forecasted highly probable foreign currency receivables.

Treatment for Time Value of Options

As outlined in Chapter 4, by applying hedge accounting under IFRS 9, entities can elect to designate only the intrinsic value of the option in the hedge relationship. Furthermore, the time value gets preferential accounting treatment and is not just posted in profit or loss. Depending on the nature of the underlying transaction, the time value is parked in equity and either capitalised into the cost on the balance sheet or released into profit or loss in an orderly fashion, reducing volatility.

The TOFA Hedging Election (Funds only)

Applying hedge accounting for certain types of funds can be a game-changer. It provides the opportunity to obtain the TOFA Hedge Election (TOFA). TOFA is a tax hedging election that reduces the volatility of timing differences caused by hedging with derivatives. Qualifying for hedge accounting and obtaining TOFA allows the designated hedges to be allocated to the capital account instead of the revenue account. Not hedging the fund's performance from FX contracts exposes the fund with offshore assets to AUD appreciation. In addition, hedging with an FX forward contract creates unwanted volatility in income distribution to unitholders if the TOFA election is not obtained. Not having a clear line of sight on investors' income can be catastrophic for some investors who rely on the income, such as retirees.

Hedge accounting provides several accounting benefits for businesses. Firstly, it helps align the accounting treatment with the underlying exposures, reducing volatility in earnings. By deferring movements on hedging instruments until they impact profit or loss, the Cash Flow Hedge Reserve allows businesses to make informed decisions without distorting the profit and loss statement. Additionally, hedge accounting offers preferential treatment for the time value of options, parking it in equity and reducing volatility. For certain types of funds, applying hedge accounting enables the TOFA Hedge Election, which reduces timing differences caused by derivative hedging and allocates hedges to the capital account, ensuring stability in income distribution to investors.

Reflecting The Impact of Risk Management Activities

It stands to reason that when an organisation proactively elects to undertake a hedging program, you expect management to reflect the risk management activities in their financial statements and financial metrics. This section will examine the significant line items that hedging will influence. We have already covered much of the additional information in the disclosures and notes to the accounts. Here, we will look at where the impacts are felt on the face of the accounts.

Offshore Revenue

The revenue or sales number is one of the key numbers in any set of financials. Let's look at the following example:

For exporters, forward contracts provide certainty of projected cash inflows that will ultimately flow into their reported income number. Organisations will also set a budget to benchmark the current year's performance against, and the offshore revenue component will be based on an FX budget rate for that income. The released gains or losses on the forward exchange contracts should be reclassified to revenue in the profit or loss statement so the offshore revenue is recorded at the hedged rate.

Capital Intensive Operator

The accounting outcome when not applying hedge accounting for a reporting entity hedging their exposure to interest rate risk would be the default treatment of FVTPL. However, the hedging instrument will likely be hedging a more material underlying position this time. This can create significant MTM positions month to month, which will distort the reported results.

However, by adopting hedge accounting and designating this as a cash flow hedge of future interest costs, we can park the gains or losses on the hedging instrument in the cash flow hedge reserve. The IRS will also have a net settlement each month or quarter, which should match the debt interest payment dates and offset the interest on the debt, which will smooth the amount of net interest expense recorded.

Cost of Inventory

One of the most critical metrics for any manufacturing business is the cost of inventory, which will impact the cost of goods sold (CoGS) and gross profit margins. For some organisations, forward contracts provide certainty of future projected cash outflows and are required when some inputs are purchased in a foreign currency. Once the underlying inventory being hedged is recorded in the books at the system rate, the gains or losses on the forward contract are moved from OCI and set against the inventory account as a basis adjustment. Ultimately, the realised gains or losses on the forward exchange contracts will adjust the CoGS line in the profit or loss statement so the gross margin reported metric is accurate and reflects the net cost of the offshore purchases after risk management activities.

When organisations implement hedging programs, the effects can be seen in various line items. For exporters, forward contracts ensure predictable cash inflows, recorded as offshore revenue at the hedged rate. Importers use forward contracts to manage cash outflows, adjusting the cost of inventory and the cost of goods sold (CoGS) to reflect the hedged rate of offshore purchases. This ensures accurate gross profit margins.

Financial Covenants

One of the primary reasons some highly leveraged companies hedge their interest rate risk is to protect their financial covenants. Although hedge accounting isn't essential here, hedging is crucial; therefore, I wanted to cover this subject briefly in this book. This section will provide general information on the main hedging covenants and some recommendations when negotiating the facility agreements in which financial covenants are included.

A financial covenant about a financing facility refers to a contractual agreement between a borrower and a lender that sets specific financial performance metrics or conditions to which the borrower must adhere throughout the loan term.

These covenants are designed to protect the lender's interests by ensuring that the borrower maintains a certain level of financial stability and meets specific obligations.

Financial covenants typically focus on various financial ratios, such as debt-to-equity ratio, interest coverage ratio, current ratio, or cash flow requirements. By setting these benchmarks, lenders can assess the borrower's ability to meet its financial obligations and monitor its financial health. Suppose a borrower fails to comply with the agreed-upon financial covenants. In that case, it can trigger an event of default, allowing the lender to take specific actions, such as demanding immediate repayment, charging higher interest rates, or enforcing collateral.

It's essential for borrowers to carefully review and understand the financial covenants before entering a financing facility to ensure they can meet the specified requirements. Failure to comply with the covenants can have serious consequences, potentially leading to financial penalties or loan defaults.

The most common one we see is the Interest Cover financial covenant. The formula for the ratio is shown below:

Interest Coverage Ratio = EBIT / Interest Expenses

Highly Leveraged Entity

The financial modelling of this company shows the base case to be stretched should the interest rate environment move higher due to their reliance on debt funding at variable rates. At current rates, they are just above the interest cover ratio of EBIT/Interest Expense = >2 in the draft financing agreement with their lenders. The lenders are concerned should future EBIT drop or interest rates increase. The borrower will be unable to meet the interest repayments, and a requirement to hedge the interest rate with an interest rate swap has been included.

In this scenario, as the CFO, you have a few options. You shouldn't just accept what's positioned without understanding the overall economics. An often neglected and misunderstood aspect of a debt financing transaction is the interest rate hedging covenants.

Spreads and bank profit could be more transparent with interest rate hedging, especially when looking at more dynamic products. So, there could be an opportunity to negotiate more favourable terms on the covenant or, indeed, the lending spreads. Banks view your relationship with them on a total return basis; consequently, if you give them plenty of business in one service line (transactional, hedging, etc.), you can use that as leverage when negotiating the terms of your new financial agreement. This is when specialised advisors can deliver a strong ROI, as they can provide the CFO with the visibility of the economics across your banking relationships so you can accurately and effectively negotiate.

In summary, it's essential to negotiate the hedging with the overall lending and, if the debt is syndicated, drive competition between the syndicate members to fight for a hedging allocation.

Summary

In Chapter 7, we explored valuable insights on how to leverage hedge accounting for improved financial reporting.

While effective in reducing risk, financial derivatives often lead to earnings volatility due to default accounting treatments. Hedge accounting solves this problem by explicitly depicting your organisation's earnings and risk profile. One practical tip is to take advantage of the Cash Flow Hedge Reserve (CFHR), which enables you to defer movements on hedging instruments until they impact profit or loss. This deferral strategy significantly reduces profit and loss (PnL) volatility, allowing businesses to make well-informed decisions without distorting their financial statements.

The chapter also underscores the preferential accounting treatment for the time value of options, an important aspect to consider. Furthermore, applying hedge accounting and obtaining the TOFA Hedge Election can be especially advantageous for certain types of funds. This election is a powerful tool for reducing timing differences caused by derivative hedging, allocating hedges to the capital account instead of the revenue account. It ensures stable income distribution to investors and protects funds with offshore assets from currency appreciation.

Lastly, the chapter provides insights into financial covenants, emphasising the importance of understanding and negotiating them with interest rate hedging.

Chapter 7 – Key Takeaways

- Harbouring volatile unrealised movements of derivatives in the cash flow hedge reserve account is a huge benefit of applying hedge accounting.
- In Australia, hedge accounting for funds is crucial in minimising income distribution volatility for unit holders.

Chapter 8:
GAAP & IFRS Compliance

Introduction

A chapter titled 'GAAP & IFRS Compliance' may sound like the most extensive section of this book. However, I'll primarily focus on hedge accounting and the presentation of derivatives in the accounts. Most of my clients struggle with these areas while attempting to comply with IFRS. Once companies understand the mechanics of hedge accounting and become familiar with posting journals periodically, their next challenge is presenting the financial report accurately. In this chapter, I will guide you through the correct way to show the numbers around financial derivatives in your balance sheet, profit and loss, and cash flow statements. I will also emphasise the importance of fair value measurement of the derivatives and the strict IFRS 13 criteria for disclosure requirements. This chapter will also provide some personal IFRS 9 hedge accounting takeaways and workarounds I have encountered over the years.

Derivative Presentation in the Financial Statements

You posted all your hedge accounting entries and completed your effectiveness testing. However, you still need to prepare your financial statements. If you are running a hedge accounting program for the first time, this section will show you the appropriate way to present your positions and gains or losses in the main reports to your financial statements. It will also cover the current and non-current reporting requirements and other presentational requirements of IFRS.

As the book covers, the default accounting treatment for financial derivatives is in FVTPL. Even the gains and losses of derivatives in a hedge relationship ultimately impact profit or loss directly or indirectly, so presentation in the PnL is as good as any place to start.

Profit of loss presentation

To comply with IFRS 9, gains or losses of derivatives not in a hedge relationship must be shown in profit or loss. The line item chosen is down to each reporting entity as the standard does not specify where it is recorded within revenue or operating profit. Whichever line item is picked needs to be repeated each reporting period. The standard setters don't want the line item to differ from one period to the next.

For financial derivatives in hedge relationships, the gains or losses recorded in profit or loss or OCI should be presented in the same line item as where the underlying hedged items are recorded. This makes sense, as you would want the offset to happen in the same place. For example, if you are hedging offshore foreign currency sales, the gain or loss on the forward contract should also be recorded within revenue, according to IFRS 9.

Cash flow statements

When preparing your cash flow statements, IFRS 9 requires the cash flows from financial derivatives in your hedge accounting programs to be recorded under operating, investing or financing activities.

Balance sheet

As per IAS 1, the rule of order of liquidity requires items to be classified and presented into current and non-current assets and liabilities. The auditors will want the split done, especially when hedge portfolios get to a significant size. This requires looking at each derivative in turn and assessing the maturity date, and if it's within 12 months, its current and any longer dates go into the non-current bucket. Most automated reporting systems for hedge accounting will produce this report for you.

Offsetting financial derivatives

This is covered in detail under IAS 32. Still, for financial derivatives, there is sometimes the ability to offset assets and liabilities in the financial statements, and in some cases, there is a 'master netting arrangement' in place. The general rule is whether there is an intention or legal right to offset them and whether they are settled net. For example, with interest rate swaps, the quarterly interest accrual on each swap is net-settled; therefore, the interest accrual in the accounts can be shown net. However, unless a Master Netting Arrangement is in place, it's inappropriate to net the asset fair value against the liability fair value of two individual swaps with the same counterparty because they are two separately legally enforcing contracts.

Master netting arrangement

The agreements are typically bilateral, and the terms will allow a netting of multiple financial derivatives. They protect one of the party's inability to fulfil their obligations on one or more of the contracts. In these cases, the reporting entity needs to disclose details of the master netting agreement in accordance with IFRS 7.

This section discusses the presentation of derivatives in financial statements, focusing on profit or loss presentation, cash flow statements, balance sheet classification, offsetting financial derivatives, and master netting arrangements. The default accounting treatment for financial derivatives is fair value through profit or loss (FVTPL). Derivatives not in a hedge relationship are shown in profit or loss, with the specific line item chosen by the reporting entity. For derivatives in hedge relationships, gains or losses should be presented in the same line item as the underlying hedged items. Cash flows from derivatives in hedge accounting programs are recorded under operating, investing, or financing activities in the cash flow statements. The balance sheet follows the order of liquidity, classifying derivatives as current or non-current based on their maturity dates. Offsetting financial derivatives depends on intention, legal rights, and net settlement, while master netting arrangements require disclosure according to IFRS 7.

IFRS 13 – Fair Value Measurement

As the fair value of a financial derivative is the starting point in so many hedge accounting entries, it's essential to look at the accounting standard on fair value measurement, IFRS 13. The fair value is not just significant for the statement of financial position and the balance sheet, but also movements in the fair values in the forms of gains or losses are crucial for the profit or loss and OCI. The financial disclosures are pretty significant, as already discussed, in terms of fair value measurement, and we will go into some of the fair value hierarchy definitions and requirements in this section.

The general objective of IFRS 13 in its application and relevance to financial derivatives is to ensure the contract has been measured by the framework laid out in the standard. The appropriate level of disclosure is added within the notes to the accounts, which provides enough information to the users to assess the appropriateness of the methods used to determine the fair value. The appropriate valuation method to select for OTC derivatives is the Income approach. This is defined as the method that will convert all future cash flows into a single present-day value. The inputs into the approach are sourced from available market information and should capture all the following:

- Estimated future cash flows

- Non-performance risk of the counterparty

- Time value of money

Bid or offer price inputs

It's common to use the mid-rates observable in the market when valuing a derivative. A reporting entity can use bid or offer rates for assets and liabilities, respectively, as an accounting policy choice. If this is true, then IFRS 13 states the entity should apply this consistently and disclose this policy in the notes.

Fair value hierarchy

Below are the three levels of categories that are part of the IFRS 13 framework, which describes the type of input used in the fair value measurement. It's important to distinguish the differences as these categories are used in the notes to the accounts. The reporting entity should always look to utilise the cleanest prices in the market, which are ranked from Level 1 to Level 3, Level 1 being the cleanest.

Level 1

These input prices are used if they relate to the same instrument you are valuing and are unadjusted. The quoted prices will be in very active markets. An example would be a listed company's share price regularly traded on one of the world's largest stock exchanges.

Level 2

These input prices are used when taking other observable market rates that don't classify as Level 1 inputs. Examples are FX spot rates provided by different central banks or interest rate fixing rates across various indices and tenors. Most financial derivatives used for hedge accounting will fall into this category.

Level 3

These input prices are used when no observable market inputs are available, or the reporting entity uses their data. Also, some inputs in observable markets that have been significantly adjusted would fall into this category. For example, the reporting entity takes the pricing that has been received from an independent broker using observable market data but then puts it through a significant adjustment using their data, which isn't visible in the market—valuations for illiquid stocks, barrier options, or private company share options and warrants.

IFRS 9 Hedge Accounting – Thinking Outside the Box

IFRS 9 Financial Instruments is an absolute beast of an accounting standard! A technical IFRS National Director of a well-known second-tier chartered accounting firm once told me she is proficient in most accounting standards. Still, IFRS 9 is the one she tends to stay away from due to its size and complexity. Hedge accounting is only a small component of the overall standard. This final section will examine my key takeaways on hedge accounting under IFRS 9 and some workaround examples for meeting eligibility criteria. Having spent ten years with a lens on the IFRS 9 hedge accounting framework, this section should provide you with a few final pearls of wisdom to use in upcoming non-vanilla hedge accounting programs.

Contrary to popular belief, the hedge accounting component of IFRS 9 is relatively small in terms of its length and prescriptive guidance. The standard has some excellent examples, but much is limited to judgment and interpretation. Due to this, over the years, there have been too many occasions to mention when a difference in the interpretation between two parties can lead to a different result regarding a specific hedge relationship qualifying for hedge accounting or not. As an advisor, I've always been on the client's side versus their auditor, trying to present the view that the hedge should qualify. In nearly all cases, when you provide adequate and compelling analysis to support your view, the auditors are usually pragmatic and more open to the hedge relationship meeting the assessed criteria. It's always better to get them involved collaboratively early on. Late, unwanted surprises at the 11th hour when there isn't the time, energy or mind space to consider an alternative view are far more challenging to get over the line. Promoting a proactive and collaborative approach is paramount. While this advice might seem common sense, it's astounding how often an "Us vs. Them" dynamic can overshadow the desire for cooperation. It's vital to recognise that auditors should maintain their independent stance, but this doesn't preclude them from sharing a common goal with the reporting entity. That shared objective is to present the financial position in the most accurate and fair manner possible, aligning with the accounting standards. Embracing this cooperative mindset can significantly enhance the audit process and foster a more constructive working relationship between auditors and the reporting entity.

For the closing credits of this book, I wanted to leave you with some of the 'tricks of the trade' and clever ways to manoeuvre around the standard to get the beneficial accounting treatment you desire.

Using internal hedges

Some larger organisations use a treasury business unit to conduct most hedging activities for efficiency gains. This can create an issue when hedge accounting is desired at each reporting entity level, as the hedge and the underlying exposure might be in separate business units. The workaround here is to create a portfolio of internal hedges that mirror the external hedge. The internal hedges will eliminate in consolidation but, at the subsidiary level, can qualify for hedge accounting. Hedge accounting at the reporting entity level is sometimes beneficial for tax and other reasons.

Inputting synthetic legs

To meet the hedge accounting criteria, the designated hedge and the exposure must have the same underlying risk to effectively offset the gains and losses. Below is an excellent example of when the underlying rates differ and how to create synthetic legs for your hedge instrument for hedge effectiveness testing. This is again a clever way to create efficiency gains and avoid using more hedging instruments than needed and hedging both sides of the price. This one is still the workaround that surprises me the most regarding getting it over the line with the auditors.

Imputing Synthetic Legs: If the underlying risk is not the same!

When a multi-national organisation is structured with a centralised treasury-hub in one location hedging the group's exposures across the many jurisdictions, this can create hedge accounting difficulties, especially at the treasury-hub reporting entity level. For example, if the currency pair being hedged doesn't contain the functional currency of the hedging business unit, this would indicate that the hedged item is likely to have a different currency exposure to the hedging instrument and thus fail the hedge effectiveness criteria. The FEC could be Sell ZAR Buy AUD, but the functional currency of the reporting entity is SGD.

A clever manoeuvre to achieve hedge effectiveness is to split the hedging instrument into two (2) legs — imputing two SGD legs. See below:

i.   Sell ZAR, Buy SGD leg, and

ii. Sell SGD Buy AUD leg

Hedged item (i) ZAR forecast receipt is subject to SGD/ZAR exchange rate movements, and hedged item (ii) the ongoing AUD costs are subject to AUD/SGD exchange rate movements. In this approach, there would also need to be two hedge items:

i.   forecast ZAR intragroup receipts from the ZAR subsidiary, and forecast AUD external operating costs out of SGD subsidiary.

The Matched Terms will then match:

Matched terms test	Hedging Instrument	Hedged Item (i)	Hedged Item (ii)	Yes/No
Notional amounts	ZAR 20000000 AUD 1641739.59	20,000,000.00	1,641,739.59	Yes
Currency	AUD/ZAR	ZAR	AUD	Yes
Inception date	24/4/2023	24/4/2023	24/4/2023	Yes
Maturity date	15/6/2023	15/6/2023	15/6/2023	Yes
Underlying risk(s)	Leg (i) SGD/ZAR Leg (ii) AUD/SGD	SGD/ZAR	AUD/SGD	Yes

Designating a pre-existing hedge

There are occasions when management decides that there is a benefit to start adopting hedge accounting midway through a hedge. For example, management has an existing book of 20 hedges executed over 12 months ago and three years until maturity. The organisation has received some tax advice, and hedge accounting is desired at each reporting subsidiary level. Contrary to popular belief, which is that the hedges need to be designated at the hedge's inception, the hedges still qualify for hedge accounting treatment! The caveat is that they are eligible for hedge accounting treatment from the date they are documented so long as they meet all the criteria. However, as the swaps will likely have a Day 1 fair value, which may be significant, this will impact the hedge effectiveness testing and embed some inherent sources of ineffectiveness in the hedge relationship. This is an example of an off-market swap designated in a hedge relationship for hedge accounting purposes.

Summary

In the final chapter, we delved into the complexities of GAAP (Generally Accepted Accounting Principles) and IFRS (International Financial Reporting Standards) compliance, focusing on hedge accounting and the presentation of derivatives within financial statements.

One of the critical pieces of advice is understanding the appropriate way to present derivative positions, gains, and losses in financial statements. It is essential to grasp the default accounting treatment for derivatives and maintain a consistent reporting approach. We also delved into vital aspects such as preparing cash flow statements and classifying derivatives on the balance sheet. I provided practical guidelines on recording cash flows from derivatives and categorising derivatives as current or non-current based on their maturity dates.

IFRS 13 is the standard that deals with fair value measurement and why fair value is so crucial for financial derivatives. The chapter underscored the objective of IFRS 13: to ensure the proper measurement and disclosure of fair values.

Lastly, I acknowledged the complexity of IFRS 9 and the importance of collaborating with auditors to ensure your hedges qualify. I shared practical strategies, including creating internal hedges within your organisation, using synthetic legs in hedge instruments, and adopting hedge accounting midway through existing hedges.

Chapter 8 – Key Takeaways

- Contrary to popular belief, the gains and losses on derivatives can be posted anywhere in the profit or loss account. However, the line item chosen should be consistent from one reporting period to the next.

- Engage with your auditor early and provide them with a hedge accounting position paper to review. Please don't give them unwanted surprises at the 11th hour.

- Prescriptive guidance in IFRS 9 is light on detail and always request a second opinion if the criteria assessment is declined. There are clever ways to navigate the standard and make it work.

Conclusion

As you've journeyed through the intricate world of hedge accounting, I hope you've understood how to effectively manage financial market risks with derivatives while maintaining accurate financial reporting. Each chapter has equipped you with essential insights, empowering you to navigate the complexities of hedge accounting confidently.

Let's recap the key takeaways that you'll carry forward:

Qualification Matters

Not all hedging instruments qualify for hedge accounting. Understanding the criteria is paramount to successful implementation.

Documentation and Strategy

Documenting your hedge accounting strategy and objectives is the foundation of your program. The Derivative Hedge Accounting Policy (DHAP) guides your application.

Audit and Compliance

Streamlining your audit process with an Audit Pack and meticulous hedge relationship documentation ensures compliance, reduces audit fees, and saves time.

Valuation and Challenges

Valuing derivatives can present challenges due to different market cuts of data and methodologies used. Distinguishing between ITM and OTM contracts and comprehending the intrinsic and time value of option valuations is crucial.

Hedge Ineffectiveness

Understanding potential sources of hedge ineffectiveness is pivotal. Quantitative testing and utilising hypothetical derivatives are crucial to minimising PnL volatility and getting testing right.

Disclosures and Reporting

Accurate and transparent disclosure of hedging activities is vital for stakeholders to assess effectiveness. Compliance with accounting standards enhances credibility.

Practical Insights

Engaging auditors early, leveraging prescriptive guidance, and strategically placing gains and losses on derivatives are practical approaches for seamless implementation.

Applying the methodologies and practices shared in this book can propel your business towards financial stability, enhanced transparency, and sustainable growth.

It's now over to you. Take the next step, apply the methodology, and witness the positive impact on your financial landscape.

Thank you for reading, and here's to your continued success.

Warm regards,

Kevin Mitchell

Glossary of Terms

A/R, A/P: Accounts Receivable and Accounts Payable, which are accounts used to track money owed to a company and money the company owes to others.

Commodity Futures: Financial contracts that allow parties to buy or sell commodities at a specified price on a future date, often used to hedge against price fluctuations.

Credit Valuation Adjustments (CVA): The adjustment made to the value of a financial derivative contract to account for the counterparty's credit risk. Applicable when the reporting entity's financial derivative position is In-The-Money.

Debit Valuations Adjustments (DVA): The adjustment made to the value of a financial derivative contract to account for changes in the credit risk of the reporting entity itself. Applicable when the reporting entity's financial derivative position is Out-The-Money.

De-designations: The process of removing hedge accounting treatment from a financial derivative contract in a hedge relationship for hedge accounting purposes.

Financial Derivatives: Financial instruments whose value is derived from an underlying asset or index, often used for risk management or hedging purposes.

Derivative and Hedge Accounting Policy (DHAP): A company's policy that outlines how it accounts for derivatives and hedges for financial reporting purposes.

Hedge Designations: Assigning hedge accounting treatment to a specific financial transaction.

Enterprise Resource Planning (ERP): Integrated software systems that help manage various aspects of a business, including financial transactions and accounting.

Earnings Before Interest, Tax, Depreciation, and Amortization (EBITDA): A measure of a company's operating performance.

Exotic Structures: Complex and non-standard derivative instruments, often used for specific risk management purposes containing optionality.

Exposure at Default (EAD): A measurement of a bank's potential loss if a counterparty defaults on its obligations.

Fair Value Through Profit or Loss (FVTPL): A classification for financial assets measured at fair value, with changes recognised in the Income Statement.

FX Forward Contracts (FECs): Agreements to exchange one currency for another at a future date at an agreed-upon exchange rate.

IFRS 13 – Fair Value Measurement: An international accounting standard that guides measuring fair value, including for derivatives and hedging instruments.

International Financial Reporting Standards (IFRS): A set of international accounting standards used for financial reporting by companies worldwide.

Interest Rate Options: Interest rate options are financial derivatives that allow investors to hedge or speculate on the directional moves in interest rates. A call option allows investors to profit when rates rise, and put options enable investors to benefit when rates fall.

Interest Rate Swaps (IRS): Agreements to exchange fixed and variable interest rate payments to manage interest rate risk.

Marked-to-Market (MTM): Valuing assets and liabilities at their current market prices.

Net Present Value (NPV): A financial metric used to evaluate the profitability of an investment or project.

Non-Vanilla Hedges: Derivative instruments that are not standard or plain-vanilla contracts, often customised for specific hedging needs.

Other Comprehensive Income (OCI): Other comprehensive income consists of revenues, expenses, gains, and losses that, according to the GAAP and IFRS standards, are excluded from net income on the income statement. Revenues, expenses, profits, and losses reported as other comprehensive income are amounts that have not been realised yet.

Re-designations: The process of modifying existing hedge accounting designations.

The Floating Leg: In an interest rate swap, the part of the swap with variable interest rate payments.

Time-period related: Matters related to the specific timeframes and horizons used in hedge accounting.

Transaction related: Matters related to specific financial transactions eligible for hedge accounting treatment.

Vanilla FX Options: Standard foreign exchange options with common features, often used for hedging currency risk.

Off-market swap: A swap where the terms differ from At-market conditions, meaning the Day 1 NPV position is not zero.

References

- BDO Australia. (2019) *IFRS 9 In Practice 2019.*
https://www.bdo.global/getmedia/367334a4-2a34-446f-8f02-f024c596ec5c/IFRS_IN_PRACTICE_screen.aspx?lang=en-GB

- CS Lucas. (2016) *Overview of Hedge Accounting: Trade Receivables.*

https://www.cslucas.com/wp-content/uploads/2023/08/Overview-of-Hedge-Accounting-Trade-Payables-Receivables.pdf

- Deloitte. (2017) *iGAAP, Drawing it together, Volume B: Financial Instruments – IFRS 9 and related Standards.* Wolters Kluwer (UK) Ltd. UK.

- Ernest & Young (2016) *International GAAP 2016, The International Financial Reporting Group of EY. Volume 3.* Wiley. UK

- Leung, J. (2015) Why the use of options as hedging instruments is more appealing under AASB 9. *Perspective.* Chartered Accountants, Australia & New Zealand.

- PricewaterhouseCoopers (2005) *IAS 39, Achieving Hedge Accounting in Practice.*
https://www.pwc.com/gx/en/ifrs-reporting/pdf/ias39hedging.pdf

Further Information & Resources

All of the downloadable resources mentioned in this book can be found here:

https://www.hedgeeffective.com/hedge-accounting/resources

The Author

Kevin Mitchell is a highly regarded hedge accounting specialist known for his exceptional ability to enhance hedge accounting programs and safeguard his clients' financial well-being. With a genuine commitment to assisting organisations in effectively managing financial risks, he established Hedge Effective Advisory, a renowned consultancy that offers expert guidance and specialised, outsourced hedge accounting services.

Kevin's extensive client list includes well-known names such as SG Fleet, Nanosonics, iNova Pharmaceuticals, Petredec, The George Institute for Global Health, Who Gives A Crap, Accolade Wines, and Adelaide Brighton. To further support his clients, Kevin has also developed Hedgehog Software, a cloud-based hedge accounting platform.

As a dedicated professional, Kevin holds memberships in industry bodies like ACCA, CA, AMCT, and ACTA. With over two decades of qualified experience and a Diploma in Corporate Treasury Management from the Association of Corporate Treasurers in London, Kevin's expertise is well-established.

Outside of his professional life, Kevin is a devoted family man with a loving wife, son, and two cherished pets. When he's not optimising hedge accounting strategies, you can find him on the golf course enjoying the occasional game and a well-deserved break.

www.kevinmitchellhedgeaccounting.com

HEDGE EFFECTIVE ADVISORY

Hedge Effective Advisory is APAC's only dedicated Hedge Accounting advisory and outsourcing partner. The team supports fellow accountants and CFOs by removing stress and time pressure from their month-end period and, most importantly, eliminating hundreds of millions in unwanted earnings volatility.

www.hedgeeffective.com

Hedgehog

Hedgehog Software is a cloud-based platform for all compliance and reporting needs. It empowers businesses of all sizes to thrive in volatile markets by providing consistent and trustworthy results. The software is also used to address the challenge of unwanted volatility in reported results due to derivative hedging, lack of internal expertise, and budget allocation concerns hindering the adoption of comprehensive Treasury Management Systems among SME-sized companies.

www.hedgehogsoftware.io

Client Testimonials

★★★★★

"We engaged Kevin to out-source the Group's hedge accounting implementation. His team have gone the extra mile to guide the Group and the external Auditors throughout the implementation – they have been continually very willing and active in providing advice."

- Adam Meehan, Petredec Pte Ltd

"The team at Hedge Effective Advisory was exceptional in providing guidance that directly addressed hedge accounting policies, including applying AASB9, documentation requirements and journal entries as applied to our swap deals. Moreover, Kevin was professional and very responsive. I highly recommend their services to anyone seeking expert advice in hedge accounting."

- Alvin Ah-Chok, Shift Financial

"I was impressed with the work that Kevin and the team did for SG Fleet in relation to our ongoing interest rate risk management. Their approach and independence ensured we had the best possible visibility of our refinancing economics and that our hedge accounting strategy was aligned with our commercial risk management objectives."

- Kevin Wundram, SG Fleet

"We are delighted with the work Kevin and the team have done for The Institute in relation to our ongoing hedge accounting requirements. Their proactive approach ensured our hedge accounting strategy was aligned to the commercial risk management objectives, resulting in minimised hedge ineffectiveness to profit or loss."

- Ganen Nadaragah, George Institute for Global Health

What Next?

Send Kevin and his team a message or book a time for a Discovery call here:

www.hedgeeffective.com/hedge-accounting/contact

Book a demo for Hedgehog Software here:

www.hedgehogsoftware.io

Contribute to raising awareness of Kevin's book and positively impact the financial community by sharing a review of 'Hedge Accounting Unlocked' on Amazon.

www.ingramcontent.com/pod-product-compliance
Lightning Source LLC
Chambersburg PA
CBHW061024220326
41597CB00019BB/3321